Staff Development: A Humanistic Approach

RUSSELL DOBSON
JUDITH DOBSON
JOHN KESSINGER

OKLAHOMA STATE UNIVERSITY

UNIVERSITY
PRESS OF
AMERICA

ISBN (Perfect): 0-8191-1131-7
LCN: 80-67254

To Mark, Mike, Susan
and Steve

iii

ACKNOWLEDGEMENTS

In the preparation of this book, the authors are grateful to many people for their assistance. They are particularly indebted to the students in their classes at Oklahoma State University, whose cooperation made possible a thorough trial of much of the newer and older materials. Special credit goes to Ms. Robin Broyles, who went far beyond her typing duties in correcting and copy editing the manuscript, to participating in developing the manuscript, by serving as researcher, advisor and a supportive friend.

TABLE OF CONTENTS

Chapter   Page

I.   THE STATE OF AFFAIRS   1

       Current Conditions.   2
         Add on Curriculum.   2
         Scientism and School Improve-
           ment   3
         Accountability and Academic
           Excellence   5
         Role Accessibility   7
         Ownership of Ideas   10
       Perceptual Baseline   11
         Personal Beliefs   13
       Organization of the Book. . . .   14
       Summary   15

II. EDUCATIONAL BELIEFS AND DECISION
     MAKING   21

       Philosophy, Values and Decisions.   24
         Beliefs and Sensitivity. . . .   27
       Why the Problem Persists.   29
         Decision Making Strategies . .   33
       A Concluding Comment.   34
       Summary   35

III. THE BELIEFS AND PRACTICES OF THREE
     EDUCATIONAL CAMPS.   41

       Historical Perspective.   42
         Design A   43
         Design B   47
         Design C   50
       The Language of Schooling   54
       Philosophy.   59
         Human Nature   59
         Nature of Learning   59
         Nature of Knowledge.   60

Chapter   Page

          Nature of Society.   61
          Purpose of Education   62
        Psychology.   62
          Human Growth and Development .   62
          Concept of Self.   63
          Human Emotions and Inter-
            personal Interactions. . . .   63
        Operational   64
          Curriculum   64
          Instructional Behavior   64
          Organization   65
          Evaluation   65
        Definition.   66
        A Concluding Comment.   66
        Summary   67

IV.   THE PERSON OF THE TEACHER.   73

        Personal Philosophy   74
          Beliefs.   74
          Values   80
        Personal Sensitivity.   84
          Feelings   85
        Personal Psychological Structure. 86
          Self Concept   87
          Personality Characteristics. .   88
          Self-Fulfilling Prophecies . .   90
          Needs.   93
        Summary   95

V.   PERCEPTUAL BASE LINE THEORY. . . . 105
        Facilitation of Awareness . . . 107
        Data Gathering Instruments. . . 110
        Schedule of Meetings. 116
        A Concluding Comment. 118

APPENDIX A -
        Educational Beliefs System
          Inventory - Part I. 123
        Educational Practice Belief
          Inventory - Part II 133

Chapter   Page

APPENDIX B -
          Directions for Scoring
          Educational Beliefs System
          Inventory and Educational
          Practice Belief Inventory . . . 145

APPENDIX C -
          Subtest Key 151

PREFACE

School environments are as different and complex as the people who live in them. Only when teachers are aware of themselves and reciprocal influences will it be possible to create atmospheres that encourage learning. Based on the assumption that the teacher is the dominant influence in the classroom, teacher self-awareness becomes a potent force in facilitating a quality climate for living and learning. Teaching involves numerous personal encounters, the outcomes of which are determined by the quality of the relationship established. The fears or insecurities many teachers have concerning their own personal or professional competencies may in fact create barriers to honest, open personal encounters with youngsters. The teacher, therefore, may assume the "role of teacher" and perceive youngsters in the "role of students" placing preconceived expectations upon themselves as well as the youngsters with whom they interact.

Each human being is, by nature, a unique person with both the creative potential and inner resources for guiding one's process of becoming and/or professional development. Yet in day to day living, many persons have turned away from themselves; they seem to have become less and less trusting of their own inner nature as the best source of determining who they are and who they may become. As a result, many persons have moved almost totally toward external determinants of self by seeking power over or from others, status and recognition. As persons become less trusting of their own inner potential and strength they come to rely more and more upon an external environment for direction in their lives. Therefore, the natural person, the genuine self with all its unlimited potential, is often lost either temporarily or permanently.

There has emerged a group of educators who have come to view a teacher's philosophy as the basis for his/her decisions about the educational process.

xi

Assuming the validity of this position, and if teachers play a significant part in establishing the educational environment, then it is important that they have some awareness of their beliefs which ultimately effect, if not determine, the climate of the learning environment. Staff and curriculum development are parallel functions. Too many promising curricular endeavors have failed because teachers were treated as passive agents in the developmental and implementation stages. Therefore, this book is committed to providing means of involving teachers in their own personal and professional development as they engage in curriculum and instruction improvement projects. If past attempts at staff development have been more frustrating than satisfying and not as successful as hoped for, then it is time to look for alternative models. Hopefully, this book provides a viable alternative.

CHAPTER I

THE STATE OF AFFAIRS

Educators have bought into the notion that
big is better, and improvement is occurring if
something different is happening in schools. If
only school personnel could be convinced to follow
this idiom then the educational system would improve and all would be well with the nation's
children. This conventional mentality has dominated the field of education for at least two
decades beginning in the early sixties and extend-
ing into the seventies. The pursuant of this
idiom resulted in a "bandwagon" approach to school
improvement.

Somewhere along the way educators seemingly
lost sight of the basic question, "What are the
reasons for schooling the young?" Activity with
the novel, unique or in some cases even with the
mystique, has served to gloss over serious entertainment or consideration of this question. Instead there is much talk about more content, more
discipline, more funds, more course offerings;
certainly the key to improvement is by doing more
of the same. And all the while big and/or more
are better, an individual school system dare not
be labeled traditional or old fashioned; attempts
must be made to remain current, up to date, and
relevant.

Where has all this led? For one thing educators have created a "paradox" and the lay public
is becoming increasingly uneasy about the quality
of education. The paradox may be simply stated:
while modern teachers and administrators are
generally more sophisticated than their counter-
parts of a decade or so ago, and while financial
aid to education has increased tremendously

1

during the same period, students are still en-
countering learning obstacles similar to those of
the past.

A perusal of the literature related to education reveals an established trend toward attempting
to minimize and/or resolve instructional and curricular difficulties through such devices as non-
graded school, open education, individually guided
education, mastery learning, computer assisted
instruction, the recent back to basics emphasis,
mainstreaming, and other grand organizational or
instructional schemes. In spite of noble efforts
at manipulating organizational, instructional, and
curricular arrangements, the school experience for
some children, remains dismal, often resulting in
failure.

From early on American educators have pas-
sionatly pursued new ideas. In an age of inex-
haustible ideas, the temptation has been and
still is to adopt new ideas indiscriminately and
apply them inappropriately. With only a superficial understanding of the basic philosophies
and theories on which innovations are based, they
often are implemented unwisely, and when expected
results are not yielded, these innovations are
rejected as hastily as first accepted. Instead
of being concerned with the question, "Why do we
do what we do?", the pragmatic posture of educators consistently brings to the forefront the
question, "How can we better do that which we are
doing?"

Current Conditions

Add on Curriculum

Alternatives generated by attempts at educational improvement have resulted in activities
that properly can be labeled as broken-fronted,
programmatic, fragmented, or topical. This type
endeavor has been employed in lieu of a comprehensive approach to school reform; that is, one
which integrates education that is basic with

2

current social concerns and social personal needs. The end result has been an add on curriculum which is exemplified by ethnic studies, drug abuse education, metric education, environmental education, and the like. These "add ons" have been an attempt to respond to current social issues and have been implemented in the hope of making the curriculum relevant.

For example, in order to make the school experience more relevant for the Black child living in the ghetto, Black Ethnic Studies are added to the social studies program. This may be current, but is it relevant to the Black child as daily life is lifed? We would agree with Cawelti (1977) who so effectively states:

> The present 'band aid' approach diverts attention and scarce resources away from what is really needed in curriculum reform -- integrating basic education with contemporary social concerns in a systematic way, -- the fear that school programs are becoming too diffuse is real (p. 3).

In any event, past staff development endeavors, program implementation efforts, and curriculum improvement procedures have been attempted in a piecemeal fashion. Integration of the schooling process, if it ever existed, has been practically eliminated by fragmentation.

Scientism and School Improvement

According to Macdonald (1968), "Training is the process of preparing a person to perform defined functions in a predictable situation, and education is the process of equipping an individual to perform undefined functions in unpredictable situations" (p. 38). An education program reflecting a training philosophy is based upon the notion that humans are the sum of their experiences . . . passive victims of their environments.

Historically, school progrms have concentrated on imparting specific skills -- that is,

3

training. Training is designed to help the trainee face situations exactly like those for which the training was designed. The aim is to prepare the trainee to perform in a predetermined manner: training seeks to make participants the same. Institutions as well as individuals are viewed from a systems perspective couched in a deficit orientation. That is, a person to be educated or a school system to be improved is seen as a problem to be corrected in order to be brought up to standard.

While training has remained as the motif for instruction, scientism is the major approach to curriculum development. Possibly, beginning with Bobbitt (1918), the field of curriculum has been greatly influenced by the goals of scientific management which have their roots in industry. The goals of scientific management in industry, based on a profit motive, were to eliminate waste and inefficiency and to maximize productivity. The concepts of cost accounting and quality control procedures being used in curricular affairs in schools today are examples of scientism borrowed from an industrial or factory model.

The influence of Bobbitt has continued through the work of curriculum theorists such as Tyler (1950), Taba (1962), Goodlad and Richter (1966) and instructional designers such as Glaser (1962), Popham and Baker (1970), Gagne and Briggs (1974) and Bloom (1976). Bobbitt's view of curriculum development and theory remains dominant. For some reason Dewey's (1916) experimentalism has had little influence on curriculum practitioners. Molnar and Zahorik (1977) noted that, whereas Tyler stressed ends before means and a linear relationship between ends and means, Dewey viewed ends and means as integrated and dialectically related. Dewey emphasized an activity before product approach; product outcomes of activity served to give meaning to and direct future activity.

The bulk of preservice and continuing education experiences of today's teachers and administrators still reflects a scientific model of curriculum and instructional development. In other words, as students, teachers' educational experiences were and are structured or patterned around a deficit or scientific model; teachers have been taught how to employ such a model while creating learning experiences for their students.

McLaughlin and Berman (1977) establish the futility of a deficit orientation in conducting inservice programs for teachers; yet this orientation remains as top priority for inservice endeavors. In reporting on the Rand Cooperation study, they noted that the deficit model is based on the assumption that problems in schools or with teachers have to do with inadequate information, inadequate skills, and so on. If these skills and information could only be imparted to teachers, then their behavior would be corrected or improved and they would be more effective in the classroom. However, school districts that have experienced success with inservice activities tend to use a developmental strategy as opposed to the deficit model. This strategy is not a single program, for the districts with successful inservice used different programs. Rather, the developmental strategy is rooted in an attitude that pervades the entire district. This attitude includes a set of expectations about the role of teachers, their professional needs, and their responsibility for solving their own problems.

Accountability and Academic Excellence

Increasingly, educators are finding themselve involved in the "minimal competency" movement as mandated by state legislation. A growing number of states have determined that students must meet statewide reading, writing, and arithmetic stand- ards before promotion or graduation. Cawelti (1977) suggests that this legislation is based o three assumptions:

1. That now promotion will serve to moti vate students to work harder.

5

2. That achievement can be legislated.
3. That schooling will be more effective
   if district resources are focused on
   specific goals with performance indi-
   cators (p. 2).

Controversy is being kindled between those
who would educate for high test scores and those
who argue for "balance" in the curriculum. The
tenth annual Gallup poll on education (1978) re-
vealed that citizens are dissatisfied with the
quality of learning taking place in the nation's
elementary and secondary schools. This dissatis-
faction, in large part, has stemmed from the well
advertised decline in scores on the Scholastic
Aptitude Test (SAT) of the College Entrance Examination Board. To educators and laymen alike,
these reports of score declines are disturbing.

Much of the lay public, and a large number
of educators, see the job of the school as quite
simple -- to help pupils learn. Priority, they
say, should be assigned to cultivation of cognitive competencies. Basic hardliners, according
to Brodinsky (1977), are proposing simplistic
demands for the so-called 3 R's with ". . .1) minimal competency, 2) proficiency testing and 3) a
performance based curriculum" (p. 524).

The popular back-to-basics movement, an out-
growth of the accountability movement, has rekin-
led enthusiasm for measurement as the way for
aluating a school system's performance and the
ablishment of credibility. Fascination with
uring what we know how to measure, those
butes that lend themselves to symbols, has
e way produced distorted vision as to what
be measured. This approach is not neces-
rong; however, it deals with only partial
l as far as human growth is concerned.
to-basics movement focuses solely on
ns do as opposed to focusing on who per-
d what they may do. This trend is a
f the input-process-output model bor-
dustry. In order for this approach

6

to school improvement to work (effectively control), human attainments are narrowly defined rather than human potentials being broadly conceived.

Additionally, it can be argued that the pressure for accountability of the schooling process has resulted in a mechanistic posture. As persons are viewed from an objective perspective, they are treated as objects. This encourages distance between and among persons (teachers, students, administrators) involved in the experience. Distancing often results in alienation. Persons in the setting perform in a robot fashion as they attempt to cope with the environment, rather than being congruent and harmonious with it.

Role Accessibility

On the other hand educators have been researching, talking and writing about human variability for many years. In fact, educators have been talking about individual differences for so long it is interesting that they still do not believe in the concept. For instance, why is it that in a school setting the concept is still reserved almost exclusively for students? Why aren't teachers as persons allowed, if indeed not encouraged, to experience the freedom inherent in the concept? Professional personnel in the school are limited by being assigned role functions, role expectations, role performance, and role criteria. Teachers and students alike bring their person to the role they assume at school. Teachers feel, teachers worry, teachers care, and teachers have different needs, wants, desires, and concerns as do students. The literature consistently concludes that the teacher is one of the most significant variables in the classroom affecting the growth of youngsters academically, socially, and emotionally. Yet little time is devoted to the study of self in teacher education curriculum at the higher education level. Research by Combs, et.al. (1974), Aspy and Roebuck (1974), Rogers (1977), and McClelland, et.al. (1978) raise serious questions about the emphasis placed on proper techniques in

7

role performance situations in parenting or teaching. If school improvement is to occur, then the uniqueness of all people, old and young, must be entertained. The quality of an institution is a direct expression of the persons who make up that institution.

We cannot legitimately continue to expect teachers to leave their person outside the door as they enter the classroom. Nor can we continue to expect teachers to be the epitome of neutrality as they don the robe and mask of the role of teacher. (Teacher role is defined as a norm with concomitant criteria that each is expected to perform.) The degree of learning experienced by the learner is contingent upon the quality of the transaction occurring within the learner as well as the interaction with his/her physical and human environments. This applies to all persons including teachers.

When people are treated according to a role instead of as unique persons, concerns for and expectations of them are quite different. For example, concerns are different for the teacher as teacher when compared with concerns for the teacher as person. Concerns for the teacher as teacher have preconceived stereotypes; performance, success, and achievement terminating in correct teacher behavior. Concerns for the teacher as person do not exclude teacher functions such as instructional behavior, but are extended to include feelings and satisfaction of the person in the role. Therefore, concerns for the teacher as person becomes a holistic approach. The teacher as teacher is seen more or less as a mind and a set of behaviors; the person as teacher is seen as mind, body, and spirit.

What one knows is important, but how one feels about what he/she knows is equally as important. The person of the teacher in the process is not only neglected, but often lost.

The concept of role behavior is based in a

rather narrow view of the nature of persons. The notion, by necessity, is derived from a static concept of human personality. Psychology has been defined as the study of behavior and attention has been focused on ways to control and direct behavior. This has led to encouragement of the homogeneity of the teaching act and the pursuit of a one best model of teaching. Combs (1978) believes that what is needed is a more comprehensive view of teaching which takes into account what is going on inside the human, not just the external manifestation or symptom. In school improvement efforts, ways must be designed for dealing with the attitudes, values, and beliefs (the internal manifestations) that persons bring to the decision making arena. Only then will there be commitment by teachers to decisions rendered about school reform.

These past attempts at improving teaching performance can be labeled "role access." Improvement is seen as increasing the number of role behaviors to which teachers in the school have access and can successfully perform. As previously stated, attempts at improvement usually result in teachers exchanging one set of role behaviors for another set of role behaviors that have been decreed as good by those in power and/or authority.

In any event, endeavors aimed at improving schooling usually begin with an analysis of what is happening before applying value judgment in arriving at what ought to occur. Base line data for this level of decision making often are obtained through a needs assessment procedure, usually a questionnaire, designed to accommodate institutional norms of the school system instead of being sensitive to persons within the school. People are seen collectively as composing an institution as opposed to the institution being composed of individual persons. For example, persons working in a factory are seen collectively as factory workers instead of being viewed as unique individuals; the same is true for school faculties.

We have no quarrel with systematic-logical

9

approaches to school reform; it is logical to begin with persons where they are in order to get them to some other place. Our concern is with the beginning point which is institutionally and role based. Need assessment procedures seek to identify the role needs of students and teachers according to institutional norms. Need assessment procedures seek to identify the role needs of students and teachers according to institutional norms. Needs which are institutionally oriented have a tendency to alienate the individual not only from the institution but ultimately from self. The real person is lost to the facade and veneer of the role he/she is expected to perform. Thus humans are rewarded for certain role behaviors instead of being rewarded for their existence and potential.

When change does occur, usually according to a preconceived model, what happens is that one set of role behaviors is simply exchanged for another set. The person in the process may or may not have changed. The procedure is based on the assumption that those in superordinate positions know more than do those in subordinate positions about what is going on. Evidence simply does not exist to establish that this assumption is valid.

Ownership of Ideas

Another nagging problem is the serious and respectful involvement of teachers in the decision making process. When teachers' needs, concerns, and knowledge base (teachers are unused experts) are treated lightly, the end result is often depressed teacher enthusiasm and creativity. The issue becomes one of ownership of ideas. When ownership of ideas is lost, the result often is alienation.

As teachers assume the role of teacher with all the predetermined, appropriate skills and behaviors, they accept an imposed reality created by the institution which may or may not match personal reality, the values and beliefs of the teacher. Consider whether or not all teachers in Germany reflected the philosophic posture of the leaders in that country during the early days of the Nazi regime.

Many teachers see schools as communities of learning as opposed to institutions of schooling. Yet due to constraints such as overcrowding, imposed expectations from without, and so on, teachers are handicapped in their attempts to implement the laws of learning. Teachers are pressured to disseminate more information in a more efficient manner, information which may or may not have personal meaning for students.

Teachers have had no choice in the <u>product before activity approach</u> that is practically mandated by most school systems. The pressure for this approach can be demonstrated by teachers being rated on a single evaluation instrument used to judge all teachers' performances according to predetermined performance criteria. The futility of a single performance scale is overwhelming when one considers Joyce (1978) has identified eighty different teaching models. The task of establishing communities of learning, where an <u>activity before product model</u> is employed, is simply too great. We see not only current procedures of making school decisions as a problem but the results of such decision making procedures are as equally great a problem.

To recapitulate, educators must come to grips with (1) ownership of ideas, (2) imposed reality vs. personal reality of teachers, (3) communities of learning vs. institutions of school, and (4) an activity before product vs. product before activity approach.

Perceptual Base Line

Any line of reasoning must begin with a set of premises, assumptions, or postulates. After considerable introspection and discourse, the authors of this book commit themselves to a particular construct relative to school reform.

11

Knowing full well that when we do so, what we have to say is based as much on what we don't know as it is on what we do know. We state this not in order to apologize, but rather to project a posture of humility which is prerequisite to scholarship. In any event we believe:

1. Schools will not improve by administrators telling teachers to shape up.

2. There is a direct relationship between personal beliefs held by the teacher and teacher practices.

3. Persons are effective in human interactions to the degree they are conscious of their philosophic beliefs and in tune with their feelings.

4. The teacher is the single most important element in the classroom setting as far as student learning is concerned.

5. The personal philosophic base of many people is one that allows them the greatest amount of inner freedom.

6. Many teachers operate from a philosophic base or combination of bases that are unknown to them; they are practicing something for an unknown reason toward a known end.

7. The most appropriate answers to questions lie within the questioner.

8. Humankind is inclined toward good and his/her nature is to seek and maintain both internal and external equilibrium.

9. Incongruence between one's behavior and philosophic beliefs often results in frustration and less effective teaching.

10. The manner in which one behaves and the choices one makes reflect one's basic attitudes, beliefs, and values.

11. Teachers have the necessary knowledge base and skills to bring about school reform.

12. Teachers can grow in personal strength and handle freedom in a rational manner.

13. The exercise of personal strength and freedom by teachers will improve the learning process for students.

Personal Beliefs

We recommend, as a beginning point for school improvement projects, the establishment of perceptual base line data dealing exclusively with personal beliefs of teachers. Due to the cumulative effect of personal beliefs of teachers on student learning, this aspect of school improvement must occur even before students needs are entertained. The perceptual base line system is a strategy designed to ascertain the degree of congruence between one's perceived philosophic beliefs and perceived day-to-day practices according to three distinct educational camps. (An indepth explanation of these three camps is presented in Chapter 3.)

The perceptual base line system is predicated upon the beliefs that: 1) there is a direct relationship between teachers' educational beliefs and their practices, and 2) a truly effective teacher is one who experiences beliefs-praxis congruency. The perceptual base line system is an approach that focuses on the uniqueness of the person of the teacher rather than on the role a teacher should play.

The literature reveals that the person of the teacher is influential in the amount and type of learning that occurs in the classroom. Inservice or preservice programs focusing on the teacher as a person facilitate teachers in dropping a role or a facade and encourage them to be with children in the educational process.

To a large degree the climate of any classroom is an expression of the consciousness level
of the teacher. The teacher generally knows how
he/she would like to interact for the good of self
and others; however, due to the imposed reality of
role expectation, they often behave in a manner
which is contrary to what they know. Any real improvement in schooling will occur only when each
person's beliefs are in harmony with his/her behaviors.

The perceptual base line system presents an
innovative approach to inservice focused upon encouraging school faculty to examine the congruency
of their educational beliefs and practices. This
approach is based upon the rationale that when
teachers' educational beliefs and practices are in
harmony, then the true person of the teacher is
released. Therefore, the perceptual base line
system of inservice is designed as a tool to use
in illuminating the person of a teacher as central
to the total schooling process.

Two instruments have been created to assist
school faculties in identifying Perceptual Base
Line Data. These are the Educational Beliefs
System Inventory and the Educational Practice
Belief Inventory (see Appendix A). The instruments identify the degree to which a person is
experiencing belief-praxis congruency. Individual
profiles for persons as well as a profile for a
total school faculty can be established. The
instruments are intended as a tool for dialogue
rather than as instruments of evaluation. An
explanation of the instruments as well as a discussion of their purpose in a Perceptual Base Line
System are Discussed in Chapter V.

Organization of the Book

In Chapter I we have attempted to present a
brief distinction between base line data, which
treats the teacher as a role, and perceptual base
line data, which focuses on the person of the
teacher. In Chapter II we attempt to establish

14

that first and foremost the teacher is a human being. This posture is a neglected phenomenon in school planning and decision making.

Chapter III deals with a classification tool for categorizing various opinions (belief systems) about the schooling process. A model for curriculum dialogue is presented to assist in discussions of school improvement.

Chapter IV is a discussion of the individual person as a catalyst for school improvement. In fact, Chapters I through IV serve to create the Perceptual Base Line Theory. Finally, Chapter V provides suggestions and strategies for using the Perceptual Base Line System in school improvement efforts.

SUMMARY

1. The "bandwagon" approach has been the dominant approach to school improvement for at least two decades.

2. Seemingly American educators have bought into the idiom that big is better and improvement is occurring if something different is being done.

3. Although teacher sophistication has improved and funding of education has increased, students still encounter learning difficulties similar to those in the past.

4. As a consequence of superficial understanding of the basic philosophies and theories on which innovations are based, new ideas are often adopted indiscriminately and applied inappropriately.

5. There is more focus on the improvement of education experiences than on understanding the educational process.

6. An "add on" approach to curriculum development has been substituted in lieu of a comprehensive approach to school reform.

7. Scientism, the major approach to curriculum development, has resulted in institutions as well as persons being viewed from a systems perspective couched in a deficit orientation.

8. Dewey's experimentalism has had limited influence on curriculum practitioners.

9. For the most part, preservice and continuing education experiences of today's teachers and administrators reflect a scientific model of curriculum and instructional development.

10. The accountability movement with concomitant behavioral objectives, need assessment endeavors and minimal competency testing is a product of scientism applied to the concept of schooling.

11. Schools as institutions focus on what persons do as opposed to focusing on who persons are and what they might do.

12. Focusing on what persons do has encouraged mechanistic answers to human problems and the viewing of teacher as a role to be performed; this discourages the uniqueness of individual persons.

13. Concern for the teacher as a person includes feelings and satisfactions of the person in the role.

14. Generally, school improvement efforts concentrate on increasing role access; that is, getting teachers to increase their repertoire of role behaviors so that they can exchange one set of role behaviors for another. Too often the person in the process is not only neglected, but lost.

15. School improvement efforts must reflect a design that takes into account the attitudes, values, beliefs, and emotions (internal manifestations) that individual persons bring to the decision making arena.

16. Imposed reality of role expectation is often in conflict with the personal reality of the individual.

16

17. Real improvement in the schooling process will occur when persons have a realistic perspective of the relationship between their philosophic stance and their teaching behavior.

18. The Perceptual Base Line System introduces a viable alternative for assisting school faculty in examining the congruency of their educational beliefs and practices.

REFERENCES

Aspy, D. and Roebuck, Flora N. From humane ideas to humane technology and back again many times. Education, 1974, 95, 163-171.

Aspy, D. and Roebuck, Flora N. Interim reports 1, 2, 3, 4. Monroe, Louisiana: National Consortium for Humanizing Education, 1974.

Bloom, B. S. Human characteristics and school learning. New York: McGraw-Hill Book Company, 1976.

Bobbitt, F. The curriculum. Boston: Houghton Mifflin Company, 1918.

Brodinsky, B. Back to the basics: The movement and its meaning. Phi Delta Kappan, 1977, 58, 522-27.

Cawleti, G. Caveats in competencies, ASCD News Exchange, 1977, 19, 2-3.

Combs, A. W., Blume, R. A, Newman, A. and Wass, H. The professional education of teachers: A humanistic approach to teacher preparation. Boston: Allyn and Bacon, 1974.

Combs, A. W. Teacher education: The person in the process. Educational Leadership, 1978, 35, 558-61.

Combs, A. W. Humanism, education, and the future. Educational Leadership, 1978, 35, 300-303.

Dewey, J. Democracy and education. New York: MacMillan and Company, 1916.

Dobson, R. and Dobson, J. S. Humaneness in schools: A neglected force. Dubuque, Iowa: Kendall/ Hunt Publishers, 1976.

Gagne, R. and Briggs, L. Principles of instructional design. New York: Holt, Rinehart and Winston, Inc., 1974.

Gallup, G. The 10th annual gallup poll. Phi Delta Kappan, 1978, 60, 33-45.

Glaser, R. Psychology and instructional technology. In R. Glaser (Ed.), Training research and education. Pittsburgh: University of Pittsburgh Press, 1962.

Goodlad, J. and Richter, M. The development of a conceptual system for dealing with problems of curriculum and instruction. Cooperative Research Project No. 45 of the U.S. Office of Education. Los Angeles: University of California, 1966.

Joyce, B. Selecting learning experiences. Washington, D.C.: Association for Supervision and Curriculum Development, 1978.

Macdonald, J. A curriculum rationale, In E. Short and G. Marconnit (Eds.), Contemporary thought on public school curriculum. Dubuque, Iowa: Wm. C. Brown Co., 1968.

McClelland, D., Constantian, C., Regaldo, D., Stone, C. Making it to maturity. Psychology Today, 1978, 12, 42-52.

McLlaughlin, M. and Berman, P. Retooling staff development in a period of retrenchment. Educational Leadership, 1977, 35, 322-25.

Molnar, A. and Zahorik, J. (Eds.). Curriculum theory. Washington, D.C.: Association for Curriculum and Supervision, 1977.

Popham, J. and Baker, E. Systematic instruction. Englewood Cliffs, New Jersey: Prentice-Hall, Inc., 1970.

Rogers, C. Beyond the watershed and where now. Educational Leadership, 1977, 33, 623-31.

Taba, G. Curriculum development: Theory and practice. New York: Harcourt, Brace World, Inc., 1962.

Tyler, R. Basic principles of curriculum and instruction. Chicago: University of Chicago Press, 1950.

CHAPTER II

EDUCATIONAL BELIEFS AND
DECISION MAKING

We believe there is value in confirmning one's personhood rather than seeking to conform to vague expectations as expressed by others of what one should be. We believe that human beings are the inventors of ideas and values and that these ideas and values are the beacons that guide daily lives and ultimately affect the degree to which persons experience self as well as others. To succumb to an imposed reality is to experience the loss or prostitution of personal ideas and values, resulting in alienation from self as well as others thus leading to role behavior which may be inauthentic. We believe that the climate of an institution is an expression of the consciousness level of the people therein and that most people know how they would like to interact for the good of themselves and others. However, due to the imposed reality of role expectation, they often behave in manners which are contrary to what they know and believe. We further believe that any real improvement in schooling will occur only when each person's practices and beliefs are in harmony. To this end this chapter is committed.

The significance of personhood in the school adventure is being illuminated by leaders in the field of education. Goodlad (1975), in his address at the 1975 Association of Supervision and Curriculum Development Annual Conference, stated:

What I am asking for is that we suspend for a time as a matter of policy our pathological preoccupation with pupil effects, as defined in statements of objectives or norm-based achievement tests. What I am asking for is that

> we concentrate, as an alternative, on
> the quality of life in the schools --
> not just for pupils but for all who
> live there each day (p. 3).

Clearly, the preceding statement is in conflict with the mentality that has encouraged the
spending of millions of dollars, under the dis-
guise of accountability, on such programs as program planning and budgeting systems (PPBS), performance based teacher education, accountability
by objectives, and minimal competency tests for
secondary school students. Educational functions
have been dominated by purpose before activity
approaches to reform. Goodlad (1978) further
states:

> Whatever the criteria applied to con-
> ducting a system of education, the
> only legitimate criteria pertaining
> to education itself arise out of the
> quality of the experience for develop-
> ing the individual. The direction
> for improving our schools is not
> doing better what we now do. Rather,
> we must begin by asking whether much
> of what we now do should be done at
> all (p. 270).

Proponents of the purpose before activities
brand of education are beginning to concentrate
more on personhood in their writings. Tyler (1977),
often referred to as the father of behavioral objectives, when asked how a curriculum syllabus of
today would compare with the now classic syllabus
he developed at the University of Chicago twenty-
five years ago, states:

> I would give much greater emphasis now
> to careful consideration of the impli-
> cations for curriculum development of
> the active role of the student in the
> learning process. I would also give
> much greater emphasis to a comprehen-
> sive examination of the non-school
> areas of student learning in developing
> a curriculum (p. 37).

22

Louise Tyler (1978), writing on curriculum evaluation holds: "My thesis is that the person is central to evaluation, that persons have the power to experience meanings that they perceive, create, discover, enjoy, and act upon" (p. 275). Tyler emphasizes the need to explore the notion of personal meaning and its significance for evaluation.

Bloom (1978), writing about school reform, states:

> Neither further opportunity for education nor increased financial support for education will do much to improve the education of each of our students. The answer does not lie in additional funds, new fads, or major and sweeping changes in the organization of our educational systems. As I see it, the solution lies in our views about students and their learning (p. 563).

Combs (1978) emphasizes a "self as instrument" concept of teaching; that is, teacher education is viewed as a problem in personal becoming. He holds that good teaching is a product of teacher beliefs or perceptions. He sees a vast difference between developing a personal philosophy and studying philosophies. He states:

> Good teaching is not, it seems, a question of right methods or behaviors, but a problem solving matter, having to do with the teacher's unique use of self as he/she finds appropriate solutions to carry out the teacher's own and society's purpose (p. 558).

Macdonald (1977) argues that values are central to curriculum work. He tends to believe that these values are derived from one's conception of the basic aims of education. He challenges curriculum theorists to make their value commitments clear. He identifies what he blieves to be two fundamental value questions: (a) "What is the meaning of human life," and (b) "How shall we live together?" (p. 20).

Rogers (1977) makes a distinction between outer and inner space as they relate to the learning experience. He states:

I believe that the next great frontier of learning, the area in which we will be exploring exciting new possibilities, is a region scarcely mentioned by hardheaded researchers. It is the area of the intuitive, the psychic, the vast inner space that looms before us. . . There is a growing body of evidence, which is hard to ignore, that shows capacities and potentials within the psyche that seem almost limitless, and that fall almost entirely outside the field of science as we have known it (p. 629).

Most of what has been done under the name of school reform and/or improvement seems to fit what rightfully can be labeled outer space as far as the person in the role is concerned. Activities focus on what is done to the teacher in order to predict and control what he/she does.

Personal being is dependent upon a harmonious relationship among the intimate self, personal self, social self and extended self. Just as a living plant grows from its roots and extends to the external world, normal human growth occurs from an intimate self, to a personal self, a social self, and ultimately an extended self. Ideally, outer space (educational environment) would accommodate or be an extension of the inner space of the person.

Philophy, Values and Decisions

Johnson (1967) suggests, "The majority of educationists, educational practicioners and scholars. . .are oriented toward improvement rather than understanding, action and results

24

rather than inquiry" (p. 127). It is apparent that educational issues are a consequence of encapsulation. That is, many individuals believe they have a corner on truth, when in fact, due to various limitations, they have only a partial and distorted perception of reality. This distortion can be the result of any number of reasons ranging from the complexity of cultural roots to the simplicity of misinformation.

The critical educational issues of our time are philosophical in nature. They have to do with questions of freedom, the nature of man, society and knowledge. Marshall (1973) establishes that educators cannot successfully achieve the objectives of refining and improving their craft until they are fairly certain of their own value orientation, the purposes and objectives that grow out of their values, and a set of criteria anchored in something deeper than the convenience of the moment or a simple hunch.

Orlich and Shermis (1965) state that teachers generally do not consciously choose a better teaching method to employ in the classroom. Rather, the teacher's temperament, the feelings of administrators, local tradition and other factors affect the teaching methods actually used. Shermis (1967) operationally reports this dilemma. He comments that any educational decision a teacher makes such as choosing a book or giving a test is in a sense affirming or denying a universe of values.

Perhaps Combs (1962) describes the comprehensiveness of this turmoil in referring to the explicit values underlying all educational practices:

> Whatever we do in teaching depends upon what we think people are like. The goals we seek, the things we do, the judgments we make, even the experiments we are willing to try are determined by our beliefs about the nature of man and his capabilities. It has always been so (p. 1).

Combs appears to build a firm case relative to the beliefs educators have acquired concerning the meaning of life. The nature and destiny of man and the nature of reality are in some way reflected in the choices that educators make.

The educator of today lives in a world in which there is confusion relative to the purposes, goals, process, and evaluation of public education. Schroder, et.al. (1973) emphasize the concern that our educational system has failed to provide students from kindergarten through graduate schools with competencies to meet the challenging problems of our ever changing society. They continue that evidence of this failure may be seen in ". . .the alienated student, the increasing gap between the objectives of educational institutions and the needs of society; and our simplistic thinking about social issues and our callous disregard for our fellowman" (p. vii).

Educational objectives are expressions of what people value, or in other words, value judgments (Tyler, 1949). Herrick and Tyler (1950) carry this position further when they state ". . .it might be more useful if the curriculum worker saw philosophy as a process for putting the whole design to work in making the important decisions on curriculum" (p. 111).

Tyler's (1949) model gives specific consideration to the concept of values since they reflect beliefs and philosophies and influence the selection of desirable behaviors. His model reflects studies of society, studies of learners, and subject matter specialists as sources of tentative educational objectives. These are filtered through a psychological and philosophical grid. Values to be retained as strong guides for behavior must be harmonious with the physical environment, the learner, the content, educational objectives, learning experiences, and evaluation procedures.

Hedges and Martinello (1977) establish that the philosophy of the school when implemented in

26

daily practice gives education wholeness, direction and purpose. Therefore, the values and assumptions comprising a philosophy of education provide the basis for practices which have integrity, consistency, and meaning to both the teachers and the learners. Webb (1977) further states, "Identity formation becomes problematic when a society loses its cohesion and becomes a mere collection of competing environments" (p. 31).

Once one accepts that in a culturally pluralistic society such as ours, there are many sets of values, the dilemma confronting educators is placed in perspective. There is no one set of values superior to all others. Consequently, diversity becomes not only inherent but encouraged. However, even diversity must proceed with some sense of common direction before a pluralistic society can survive. Tyler (1949) establishes four fundamental questions to be used in planning a program of curriculum and instruction.

1. What educational purposes should the school seek to attain?
2. What educational experiences can be provided that are likely to attain these purposes?
3. How can these educational experiences be effectively organized?
4. How can we determine whether these purposes are being attained? (p. 1).

Tyler makes no attempt to answer these questions. The answers, of course, will vary to some extent from one level of education to another and from one school to another because of differing values and beliefs.

Beliefs and Sensitivity

For at least fifty years, there has been a progressively widening split in the ranks of persons concerned with the purposes and processes of education in the United States. This split has profoundly affected trends in both theory and practice.

27

Shane (1973) reports that the so-called Scientific Movement in education which became apparent in the 1920's was one of the indications of the developing schism. This movement emphasized content, minimum essentials and a reliance on normative type tests. He continues that this emphasis on testing was, of course, in direct conflict with the more humanistic ideas which were embodied in the beliefs of the Progressive Education Association.

The opposing factions can be classified by saying that one group of educators emphasize a command of selected responses and mastery of predetermined content as a goal for schooling. Another group of educators emphasizes that education should place greater focus on human development, self-realization, and social reconstruction.

Since the early 60's there have been a growing number of educators who are advocates of a narrowly defined concept of educational objectives and practices. These persons are concerned with efficiency in school programs which is based on systems designs, behavioral objectives, performance contracts, and competency based instruction. Ideologically these concepts are in direct conflict with humanistic beliefs.

It is obviously a gross understatement to say that educators do not agree on the purpose of schooling. Some opt for cultivation of intellectual skills. Still others bemoan the neglect of values, attitudes and other affective dispositions.

No small wonder that Ebel (1972) raises two questions relative to the purpose of schooling. "If the schools are to be accountable for the performance of their pupils, the question that immediately arises is, what performance?" "What should be the relative emphasis placed on affective dispositions as opposed to cognitive capabilities?" (pp. 3-4).

28

Perhaps in a multi-valued culturally pluralistic society there should be no final answer to
the question, what is the purpose of schooling?
Rather, what is needed is that the question not
be placed in the back closet, but be constantly
entertained. Maybe there is value in goals that
are implicit rather than explicit.

Why The Problem Persists

It appears that teaching has detoured from
an almost obtained goal of professionalism to an
out and out occupation. There are probably in-
numerable reasons for this current state of the
art. Many, if not most teachers have come to see
their teaching assignments as a job, due to the
degree of powerlessness and hopelessness they
have experienced over the years. Nothing is more
depressing than to be constantly encouraged or
coerced, whichever the case may be, to implement
decisions that one was not involved in making.
This lack of involvement over the years has
served to depress teacher enthusiasm and vitality.

The power elite model of decision making is
prevalent in today's schools. This model is a
down-the-line technique of making and implementing decisions. An example of this model would be
a principal who arbitrarily decides that most of
his/her teachers have sloppy chalkboard posture.
An inservice program is designed and implemented
to improve chalkboard posture. Teachers are
coerced into attending an inservice activity on
"chalkboard posture," then they are expected to
adopt the new posture. Chalkboard posture becomes an item on the teacher evaluation form and
in order to gain reward, teachers demonstrate
this new behavior. The trauma of this type
experience is increasingly a part of the dysfunc-
tional aspects of educational planning. Although
there is much to be learned about what happens
when attempts are made to change the school, what
is clear is that attempts never quite result in
what was anticipated or expected. The outcome,
after the initial flurry settles, is that very

tired and disillusioned teachers and administrators usually revert to their original mode of organization and concomitant behavior.

One is led to question if any real change can ever occur under the current bureaucratic structure (power-elite) or organization. Bureaucracies bless superordinates with rights and saddle subordinates with obligations. This type structure might work in profit motive institutions, but can it be applied effectively to institutions with a social motive? In profit motive institutions workers have an occupation or job; while in social motive institutions such as hospitals and schools there are many workers who are professionals. Further, a bureaucratic organization encourages formalistic impersonality, an attmept to separate organizational duties from the private lives of employees. As teachers continue in their efforts toward professionalism and their status increases, efforts at school change will continue to be dampened. Abbott and Lovell (1965) predict ". . .that the educational administrator of the future will be more like the hospital administrator and less like the industrial tycoon, who appears to be our model today" (p. 49). Quality leadership is determined by the number of personalities enhanced not by the number of persons dominated. Innovations as a tool to enhance the personal status of those in administrative posts hopefully will become a thing of the past.

The cause of anything is everything. To be able to attend to the complexities presented by the world to an individual's perceived environment is not only impossible but probably undesirable as far as maintaining any degree of equilibrium. The individual person is blessed by selected perceptions. What causes (allows) an individual to be attentive to certain stimuli at certain times? Personal reality, not imposed reality, is what counts. Things are pretty well the way they seem depending on who is doing the "seeming."

Hall (1975), in dealing with this phenomenon

states:

> However certain aspects of our world
> are of higher priority. Some appear
> to leap out at us, demanding our atten-
> tion. How we perceive these things is
> dependent on the unique and multifaceted
> person that each of us is, as well as
> the characteristics of the issue, idea
> or thing that is the center of atten-
> tion (p. 3).

Our thesis emphasizes that personal desires
which are internally based will result in positive
lasting growth, and the externally based demands
will diminish soon after the external stimuli is
removed. Unless internally based concerns, wants
and desires are included in inservice activities,
the result is a waste of dollars.

The research efforts of Newlove and Hall
(1976) relative to teacher concern and innovation
is to be applauded. We believe that their efforts
are at least a "cut above" the current needs
assessment approach. To deal with teacher concerns seems to be more personal and human than
dealing with teacher needs. Needs are usually
externally determined and role oriented; concerns
are usually internally expressed and personally
oriented. However, their work falls short on at
least two counts. First, teacher concerns about
innovations are still focusing on the person
(teacher) as a role and the concerns are limited
to innovations (institutional emphasis). This
reinforces Abbott's view of formalistic impersonality. Second, the concerns are treated in such
a manner as to fulfill obligations that have been
institutionally determined. Bureaucracy is accepted
as a given. The basis for teacher as person concerns are never really considered as a part of
their practitioner efforts.

The importance of values in educational decision making can be demonstrated by value words,
such as goals, objectives, adequate, greatest

importance. Abstractness is assigned to values and educators for some reason refuse to come to grips with them. First of all we do not believe that values are so abstract and illusive that teachers cannot grasp their place in the schooling process. Educators cannot afford the luxury of continuing to ignore this concept in educational planning and decision making. We submit that the very heart of educational planning and decision making is value based through value goal setting and values clarification. Declared value systems provide guidelines for planning for the future. To attempt to forecast, predict or engage in long range planning while ignoring the values base of those involved and affected by the decisions, is to plan for failure.

We do not mean to imply by this discussion that values are totally neglected in educational planning; for certainly, any school policy manual sets forth noble goals for human direction. However, we submit that this aspect is treated in a casual manner. Educators seem to assume that everyone knows the values so there is no point in wasting time with exploration. What happens very often is that what everyone seems to know, no one knows.

We are convinced that teachers behave according to their philosophies of life. Contained within or associated with this philosophy are values, beliefs, and attitudes. Beliefs/philosophy whether clearly known or not, keep individuals on track toward goals and determine the quality of interaction with others. When individuals are consciously aware of their beliefs, they can serve to facilitate positive growth.

The philosophies of individuals within an institution collectively serve to contribute heavily to the philosophy of that institution. Different schools value different things. We submit that it is not only desirable, but absolutely crucial if meaningful direction is to emerge, that individuals within an institution have a crystal clear grasp of

32

their basic beliefs relative to human nature and have cognizance of how these beliefs are translated into their teaching role or school activities. Different beliefs reflect and demand different behaviors.

Decision Making Strategies

Due to the nature of schooling, the hustle-bustle to get the job done and improve upon it while doing so, teachers simply are not given sufficient time and assistance in thinking through beliefs and clarifying values. Instead, as was established earlier in this chapter, educational goals and objectives are arrived at in a rather haphazard fashion without adequate investigation and understanding. (The art of philosophizing has never gained respect in educational decision making in America although in reality, it is the soul or basis for all educational planning and certainly for those that deal with curriculum and instruction.) Goal setting without declared philosophical underpinnings is analagous to a ship at sea without a compass. As nearly as we can tell, current school planning falls into five categories: 1) Rearrange the deck-chairs on the Titanic, 2) Betty Crocker approach, 3) Diet approach, 4) Candy Store approach, and 5) Wet-Finger approach.

Rearrange the Deck-Chairs on the Titanic Syndrome. In this approach variables, usually organizational, are constantly manipulted in attempts to improve the schooling experience. The entertainment of one or two schooling variables at the neglect of others does not produce what is expected. This approach denies the interrelatedness of all things; that is, all the variables that compose the system of schooling. We submit that it is no small wonder educational research literature is full of "no significant difference" studies.

Betty Crocker. In this approach the emphasis is definitely on improving what is currently happening. The strategy is to treat teachers as technicians and to provide them with a cookbook of recipes to improve their craft.

Diet Approach. This approach is analogous to the obese person who selects the most desirable foods from among several diets and then wonders why no progress is being made toward the goal of losing weight. The diet approach to curriculum improvement has educators selecting isolated programs from among the many available, implementing them indiscriminately, and wondering why the children and teachers are not achieving the stated goals.

Candy Store. Imagine a young child in a candy store, with a small amount of money, trying to decide which combination of candies to purchase. Educators are consistently bombarded with foolproof educational programs which proclaim fantastic results. Without a concise philosophical base from which to make decisions, often the decision is made according to that program which seems most attractive at the moment or has the most gregarious sales person.

Wet Finger. This approach is similar to the old "pendulum swing" approach. Symbolically, the educator extends his/her wet finger into the air to determine the direction of the wind. The end result of this approach amounts to chasing educational "band wagons."

A Concluding Comment

We have come to believe that the most practical and critical aspect of schooling and teaching is that one has a synthesized philosophy of values, clarifies choices, and increases consistency or congruency with one's day-to-day practices. To this end, one can celebrate freedom; that is, exercise control over one's environment in a responsible manner.

Likewise, when members of a group, through

honest interaction (patient discussion and listening) develop a shared philosophy, they have guidelines or a foundation from which to examine variables such as curriculum, organization, instruction, evaluation, school mission, and society. An identified, hopefully shared, philosophy enables a faculty to order priorities, establish goals, identify activities, analyze conflicting proposals, and to convert (by nurturing) controversy into meaningful school experiences. Lewis (1975) defines philosophy as ". . .a coherent and consistent organization of beliefs and values, which is a necessary tool in order to choose, define, and organize the goals and objectives for the school" (p. 111).

Chapter V explains a process, through on-site conferences, designed specifically to assist a school faculty in clearly identifying their beliefs relative to human nature and how these beliefs are translated into educational specifications. This is the Perceptual Base Line System. The goal of such an activity is that the schooling process reflect beliefs-praxis congruency. Then and only then will teachers shed the role of walking-talking technicians and function as professionals.

SUMMARY

1. Imposed reality contributes to the loss of ideas which often results in alienation; in order to cope the individual adopts role behavior which may or may not be authentic.

2. Real improvement in schooling will occur when each person's beliefs, feelings, and behavior reflect congruency.

3. Educational leaders (Goodlad, Tyler, Bloom, Combs, Macdonald, Rogers) are stressing that the person is central to the educative process.

4. Arriving at concensus relative to the purposes of schooling is a complex affair in a society

35

that purports to encourage pluralism.

5. Educational practicioners are more oriented toward implementation and improvement rather than theoretical/philosophical issues underpinning the implementation.

6. The critical philosophical issues of education have to do with questions of freedom, the nature of humans, and the conditions of society.

7. Educational choices of today shape the practices of tommorow.

8. Distinct camps of educators can be distinguished relative to their beliefs about the purposes and processes of schooling.

9. The bureaucratic structure of schools limits teacher involvement in decision making relative to school activities.

10. When members of a group (school faculty) are consciously aware of a philosophy, they have a foundation for assessing their current daily practices.

11. The Perceptual Base Line Theory is a tool that individuals as well as groups can use in examining theory/philosophical practice consistency.

REFERENCES

Abbott, M. and Lovell, J. (Eds.). Change perspectives in educational administration. Auburn, Alabama: School of Education, Auburn University, 1965.

Bloom, B. New views of the learner: Implications for instruction and curriculum. Educational Leadership, 1978, 35, 563-76.

Combs, A. W. Teacher education: The person in process. Educational Leadership, 1978, 35, 558-61.

Combs, A. W. (Ed.). Perceiving behaving becoming. Washington, D.C.: Association for the Supervision and Curriculum Development, 1962.

Ebel, R. What are schools for? Phi Delta Kappan, 1972, 54, 3-7.

Goodlad, J. Goodlad urges improved quality of life in schools as prime goal. ASCD News Exchange, 1975, 17, 1-12.

Goodlad, J. On the cultivation and corruption of education. The Educational Forum, 1978, 42, 267-78.

Hall, F. Concerns about the innovation: What are they? In B. Newton, G. Hall (Eds.), A manual for assessing open-ended statements of concern about innovation. Austin, Texas: Research and Development Center for Teacher Education, The University of Texas at Austin, 1976.

Hedges, W. and Martinello, M. What the schools might do: Some alternatives for the here and now. In L. Berman, J. Roderick (Eds.), Feeling, valuing and the art of growing, Washington, D.C.: Association for Supervision and Curriculum Development, 1977.

Herrick, V. and Tyler, R. Toward improved curriculum theory. Supplementary Educational Monograph, No. 71, Chicago: University of Chicago Press, 1950.

Johnson, M. Definitions and models in curriculum theory. Educational Theory, 1967, 17, 125-29.

Lewis, E. (Ed.). A discussion guide to initiate study of educational philosophy and goal setting. Sacramento: California School Board Association, 1975.

Marshall, J. The teacher and his philosophy. Lincoln, Nebraska: Professional Educators Publications, Inc., 1973.

Macdonald, J. Values, bases and issues for curriculum; in A. Molnar and J. Zaherik (Eds.), Curriculum Theory. Washington, D.C.: Association of Supervision and Curriculum Development, 1977.

Newlove, Beulah and Hall, F. A manual for assessing open-ended statements of concern about an innovation. Austin, Texas. The Research and Development Center for Teacher Education. The University of Texas at Austin, 1976.

Orlich D. and Shermis, S. The curriculum: Attitudes and problems in the pursuit of excellence: Introductory reading in education. New York: American Book Company, 1965.

Rogers, C. Beyond the watershed and where now. Educational Leadership, 1977, 35, 623-31.

Schroder, H., Karlins, M. and Phares, J. Education
for freedom. New York: John Wiley & Sons,
Inc., 1973.

Shane, J. "Foreward" in Reschooling society: A
conceptual model. by J. Macdonald, B. Wolfsen,
and E. Zaret, Washington, D.C.: Association
for Supervision and Curriculum Development,
1973.

Shermis, S. Philosophic foundations of education.
New York: American Book Company, 1967.

Tyler, Louise. Curriculum evaluation and persons.
Educational Leadership, 1978, 35, 275-279.

Tyler, R. Basic principles of curriculum and instruction. Chicago: University of Chicago
Press, 1949.

Tyler, R. Desirable content for a curriculum
development syllabus today. In A. Molnar and
J. Zahorik (Eds.), Curriculum theory. Washington, D.C.: Association of Supervision and
Curriculum Development, 1977.

Webb, R. Youth life-worlds and the American culture. In L. Berman and J. Roderick (Eds.),
Feeling, valuing, and the art of growing,
Washington, D.C.: Association of Supervision
and Curriculum Development, 1977.

CHAPTER III

THE BELIEFS AND PRACTICES OF
THREE EDUCATIONAL CAMPS

Two thousand years ago the Stoic philosopher Epictetus wrote, "Men are disturbed not by things, but by the vision which they take of them." In a time when educators are continuously concerned with finding better ways of doing what they are doing, and citizens are eager to hold them accountable for this, is it not time to reassess the purposes of schooling, if indeed such purposes can be identified? Ebel (1972) states:

> We seem to have lost sight of, or become confused about, our main function as educators, or principal goal, our reason for existence. We have no good answer that we are sure of and can agree on to the question, What are schools for? (p. 3).

Answers to the question posed by Ebel will probably vary, as Myers (1976) so succintly states: ". . .depending upon whether one is a Communist or Capitalist, Idealist or Pragmatist, old or young, rich or poor, a citizen of an undeveloped or a developed country. Surely, Socrates, Horace, Kant, Spinoza. Tolstoy, Satre, Russell, Rousseau, and Freud would disagree" (p. 3). Deciding on the purposes of schooling requires responses to complex questions for which there are probably no best answers.

There is a crucial need for "languaging"--a way of talking about schooling without arguing. The Spanish philosopher, Gasset (1967), establishes:

> The words of language have their meaning imposed by collective usage. Speaking is a re-using of that accepted meaning,

41

saying what is already known, what
everyong knows, what is mutually
known (p. 60).

If one is to pursue his/her roots of reality relative to the purposes of schooling he/she must un-
cover meanings of words and concepts blurred by
custom and usage. "This will require 'revivifying'
or 'resucitating' the meanings" (Frazier, 1970,
p. 23).

Certainly in a democracy, with a pluralistic
or multi-value base, there is a need for a communication vehicle that will assist individual persons
as well as publics in approaching concensus in establishing congruence among their beliefs and practices concerning the schooling of the young.
Responsible persons can ill afford to leave this
chore to the persuasive powers of a few.

From a historical perspective it is no surprise
that in a troubled society some will seek a national
solution through the schools. Let us recapitulate.
There is a progressively widening split in the ranks
of persons concerned with purposes of the school
experience, a split that has resulted in definite
trends in both beliefs and practices.

Historical Perspective

What is the state of school reform? Our spec-
ulation is that the division among educational camps
will sharpen and that the self-appointed priests
of the various camps will extol their brand of philosophy and practices in a rhetorical fashion. From
our perspective it is as equally important to know
why we do what we do as it is to be good at what
we do.

For purposes of clarity, we have combined the
numerous philosophic camps into three categories.
This is done with awareness of the pitfalls of
labeling and the absurdity of dealing with complex
affairs with an either/or mentality. However, we
believe this simplistic explanation will expedite

42

the discussion and aid in providing an historical perspective leading to contemporary educational thought. We have labeled the three educational camps Design A, B, and C, respectively. Design A educators are essentially 'Skinnerian' in belief, Design B advocates subscribe to the 'John Dewey' type philosophy, and Design C followers generally are champions of those beliefs espoused by Carl Rogers.

Design A

Curriculum development according to Design A is psychologically couched in Behaviorism and philosophically based in Essentialism. Behavioristic investigation is limited to objective, observable phenomena and to the methods of natural science. Essentialism mediates between the Realist and Idealist philosophical extremes. Marshall (1973) contends that Essentialists believe that ". . .some essentials, like the three R's, resting on established knowledge and tradition must continue to be taught as the indisputable core of curriculum" (p. 97).

According to Bigge (1964), the American psychologist, J.B. Watson leaning heavily upon the research of Pavlov, formulated behaviorism around 1913. Watson proposed to make psychology scientific by utilizing objective methods, including adaptations of Pavlov's conditioning techniques, investigations of human physiology, the study of animal behavior and laboratory experiments.

Watson, who was an animal psychologist at Johns Hopkins University, objected to the concept of introspection, which he considered unscientific. Sargent and Stafford (1965) state that Watson believed psychology's real concern was to study behavior, not consciousness.

At this same period in history, Edward L. Thorndike was formulating his theory of learning called S-R bond or connectionism (Bigge, 1965). Thorndike (1912) assumed that through conditioning,

43

specific responses come to be linked with specific stimuli. Thorndike's laws (1912, 1913, 1949) leave no room for thought or insight and apparently do not require any kind of purposiveness of man nor of lower animals. It is Thorndike's name that is generally associated with the concept of trial and error.

Eisner (1977) eloquently describes Thorndike's influence on current school practice:

The general aspiration that Throndike held for schooling was in the creation of a science of educational practice. Through experimentation it would be possible, he believed, to discover the laws of learning so that teachers could rely not upon intuition, chance, or talent, but upon tested principles and procedures for managing the student's learning (p. 9).

According to Sargent and Stafford (1965), Thorndike contributed to practically every branch of psychology and has become famous for his work in learning and intelligence testing. Eisner (1977) agrees and states that Thorndike has been one of two men who have definitely influenced the direction of inquiry into education. Thorndike's works not only pervade the development of the field of educational psychology but also were related in textbooks used by most teachers, counselors and school administrators. More specifically, Thorndike's research has had a tremendous impact upon current educational practices such as the popularization of standarized testing, accountability, and an emphasis upon teacher skills, strategies or techniques, to mention a few.

The leading proponent of Behaviorism today is B.F. Skinner. Goldenson (1975) states that Skinner conducted the first systematic study of operant conditioning in 1938 and he and his associates have continually refined the process labeled behavior shaping. According to Skinner practically every detail of our behavior and children's behavior is shaped by reward and punishment in one form or another. Programmed learning is a relatively recent application of Skinner's operant conditioning/behavior shaping.

Sulzer and Mayer (1972) emphasize that due to the influence of Skinner, there has been an increased interest in ". . .basic behavioral laboratory research as well as applied research in settings such as schools. . ." (p. 2). Their book (one of many to reflect the influence of Skinner) is written on the basic assumption that what students do is of primary importance. They continue that behavioral change is implicit in any school program and that ". . .the decision is not whether behavior should be changed, but who will change it, what the goals will be, and which specific program of behavior change will be used" (p. 3). They herald empirical evidence as the basis upon which educational methods will become increasingly precise and effective.

Therefore, the teacher, counselor or school administrator adhering to the tenets of Behaviorism becomes a behavioral engineer (Dimick & Huff, 1970). The behavioral engineer, through the scientific application of empirically validated principles not only brings about behavior modification in children but also manipulates environmental conditions so that the child can function optimally as defined by an outside authority.

The Essentialist policy in American education is made up of Idealism and Realism. Idealism as a school of thought began with Plato, often considered the Father of Idealism (Marler, 1975). The thinking of Descartes and Spinoza added to this particular philosophy. During our country's colonial period, Calvinist Johnathan Edward and Samuel Johnson emphasized the discipline of the mind as the instrument of gaining knowledge. During this same period, Immanuel Kant and George Hegel, among others, contributed to this particular school of thought. The man generally regarded as the Father of Modern Idealism is Bishop Berkeley.

Aristotle is considered the Father of Realism. However, John Locke, Johann Herbert, Alfred North Whitehead, Bertrand Russell and George Santayana are some of the more notable contributors to this particular philosophic thought. The Realism movement provided much of the philosophical basis for the school testing movement and the development of educational psychology. The intelligence scales of Binet and Terman and the measurement of curricular and instructional variables pursued by Thorndike and his successors have their roots in Realism.

The melding of Idealism and Realism extremes seems to produce Essentialism. Kneller (1964) identifies four fundamental principles which provide the bases of the Essentialist movement. First, learning involves hard work and often unwilling application. Emphasis is placed on the importance of discipline. The child attains personal control only through voluntary submission to discipline, imposed by the teacher. Second, the initiative in education lies with the teacher rather than the pupil. Third, assimilation of prescribed subject matter is emphasized. A fourth principle stresses that the school is obligated to retain traditional methods of mental discipline. Creative achievements of the past are sources of knowledge for dealing with problems of the present.

Therefore, a teacher, counselor or school administrator who aligns with the Essentialist philosophy believes that the purpose of education is both intellectual and moral discipline. The purpose of education from the standpoint of society, ". . .is to transmit the essential portion of the total heritage to all who come to school" (Wingo, 1974, p. 61). The curriculum is an ordered series of subject matter, intellectual skills, and essential values. The teacher, of course, is the active agent of this transmitting process. The school has the role in society of ". . .preserving and transmitting the essential core of the culture and incidentally to the ordered evolutionary process of change" (p. 62).

Design B

Education by Design B is based on Cognitive-field psychology and in Pragmatism and Experimentalism, schools of educational philosophy. Marler (1975) states that Pragmatism as a formal school philosophy is a modern movement which originated in the intellectually and socially turbulent years at the end of the nineteenth and beginning of the twentieth centuries.

The cognitive-field theory of psychology is based upon the thinking of Kurt Lewin (Bigge, 1964). This psychology represents a relativistic, as opposed to an absolutistic, mechanistic manner of viewing man. "The basic principle of relativism is that nothing is perceivable or conceivable as a thing-in-itself" (Bigge, 1964, p. 176). Therefore, relativism means that psychological reality is defined in subjective, perceptual terms and not in objective, physical terms. From this definition then, a person's ". . .reality consists of what one makes of that which one gains through one's senses or otherwise" (Bigge, 1975, p. 176).

The heart of Lewin's psychological pursuits centered in the motivating conditions of person-environment situations. He stressed democratic ideals and practices.

Jerome Bruner (1960) is also considered to be a cognitive-field psychologist. He conceptualized the "spiral curriculum" which emphasizes that children can learn at their own level any subject matter at any age and that educators can settle for incomplete, intuitive understanding at intermediate stages of learning. Bruner believes that full knowledge and understanding come with repeated attacks, at increasingly mature levels, on the same topics. The concept of categorizing behavior has been studied by Bruner, Goodnow, and Austin (1957). Bruner (1957) introduced the term "coding system" to describe that the organism learns to code situations which are encountered and that this may lead to appropriate behavior in relation to them. Therefore, all problem-solving behavior implies that the problem has been in some way coded. Bruner proposes that those coding systems should be taught which permit the greatest application to the solving of new problems.

Cognitive development, according to Piaget, is the intellectual counterpart of biological adaptation to the environment. Wadsworth (1971) explains that as individuals adapt biologically to their environments they also adapt intellectually and that individuals organize and give structure to their external worlds through assimilation and accommodation. Adaptation begins at birth with the exercise of sensory-motor reflexes, but as children develop, the adaptations they make are increasingly less related to sensory and motor behaviors alone.

Piaget (1967) stressed that knowledge is not transmitted directly but is constructed. He states:

The clearest result of our research on the psychology of intelligence is that even the structures more necessary to the adult mind, such as logico-mathematical structures, are not innate in the child; they are built up little by little. . . There are no innate structures: every structure presupposes a construction. All these constructions originate from prior structures and revert in the final analysis. . .to the biological problem (pp. 149-50).

Therefore, the teacher, counselor or school administrator adhering to the tenets of cognitive-field psychology place great emphasis upon the individual and interactions with his/her environment. Providing sequential, growth-producing experiences for all students is of great import in the school based in Design B. Democratic values are stressed in order that students become productive citizens in their adult years.

Pragmatism basically represents an American

philosophical development although parallel ideas were presented by England's Schiller and Balfour and German's Vaihinger. The forerunner of pragmatic thought can be found in Heraclitus, a Greek philosopher who emphasized the constancy of change; in Sophists, who denied the possibility of knowing ultimate reality; and in Quintilian, the Roman who emphasized action rather than deductive reasoning as a pathway to learning.

In America, the focus of Pragmatism was the harmonizing of the individual and society. The work of William James caught the attention of John Dewey who is considered the Father of Experimentalism, a branch of Pragmatism. Dewey professed that the process of education provided the proper testing ground for philosophical theory; his works emphasized the individual and stressed activity for activity's sake, rather than for evaluation. Dewey (1938) asks: "How shall the young become acquainted with the past in such a way that the acquaintance is a potent agent in appreciation of the living present?" (p. 23).

Some of the basic tenets (Dawson, 1976) associated with this particular philosophy of education are:

1. The importance of individual differences and interests of students.
2. Providing alternatives so that the student has the opportunity to experience freedom of choice and the concomitant responsibility.
3. The stressing of the scientific method of thought and learning.
4. Knowledge is considered to be based in experience.
5. Truth is relative; the ultimate questions of life cannot be answered as absolutes or fixed truths.
6. Students' psychological needs are paramount over the logical order of subject matter.
7. Values are instrumental.

Therefore, the teacher, counselor or school administrator adhering to the tenets of Pragmatism/ Experimentalism provides an activity-centered curriculum in which choice is inherent and problem solving is prized. Emphasis is placed on individuals and their needs. When needs are met growth continues and therefore, the individual progresses toward the realization of his/her potential. Education must serve as a source of new ideas for enriching society.

Design C

Education by Design C has its roots in Humanistic psychology and Existential philosophy. Humanistic psychology focuses on "man himself - his needs, his goals, his achievements, his success" (Goble, 1970, p. xii). The human potential movement is often referred to as the Third Force and has become a voice in education that is beginning to be heard over the cries of the technologists, portrayed in Design A and those of the Experimentalist, depicted in Design B.

Abraham Maslow, Rollo May, Fredrick Perls, Arthur Combs, and Carl Rogers are probably among the most notable psychologists associated with Humanistic psychology. According to these persons, the single basic motivation of all human beings is the actualization of one's potentials (Patterson, 1973). An individual's specific needs are organized (Maslow, 1979) and assume temporary priority relative to this basic need for self-actualization. A specific need which is temporarily most important receives attention or becomes the figure against the ground of other needs, to use Gestalt terminology.

Therefore, the concept of threat becomes very important in the learning process. Humanistic psychologists believe that threat leads to resistance to change; that threat will not lead to self-enhancing behavior, but to self-preservative behavior. According to Combs and Snygg (1959) learning or positive behavior does not occur under threat, and, therefore, it becomes increasingly important to consider those conditions which minimize threat and which lead to positive behavior change.

Rogers (1957, 1961) has delineated conditions or aspects of personal relationships which minimize threat or the need to protect oneself and which, therefore, maximize self-enhancing behaviors. Three of the basic conditions are: 1) empathic understanding, 2) respect or nonpossesive warmth, and 3) genuineness. A brief description may clarify for the reader the meaning of these conditions. Empathy, according to Rogers (1961), is ". . .to sense the (other's) private world as if it were your own, but without losing the 'as if' quality. . ." (p. 284). The Cherokee Indians are credited with a prayer that expresses the concept of empathy. The last phrase is: ". . .have walked the trail of life in his moccasins." Empathy, therefore, is the ability and the sensitiveness to consider things from another's point of view.

Nonpossessive warmth or respect is a second condition necessary for minimizing threat and maximizing self-enhancing behaviors. Inherent in this concept is an acceptance of the other as a person of worth without judgment. Patterson (1973) sums up the meaning of nonpossessive warmth as: "Thus one may accept and respect a person as a person, but still not agree with or condone all of his behaviors" (p. 71).

Genuineness connotes openness, honesty and sincerity. Rogers (1957) states that a genuine person is freely and deeply himself and that, therefore, he is without a facade. Jourard (1964) uses the term transparent in discussing genuineness. Many Existential philosophers refer to the genuine person as one who is authentic.

Rogers (1977) discusses the fundamental conditions that may be observed when person-centered learning develops in a school. He states:

51

The political implications of person-centered education are clear: the student retains his power and control over himself; he shares in the responsible choices and decisions; the facilitator provides the climate for these aims (p. 74).

Maslow (1956) has identified fourteen characteristics that self actualized or fully matured persons have in common and which differentiates them from other people. These are:

1. A greater awareness of their environment.
2. An acceptance of self, others and nature.
3. Spontaneity.
4. A sense of responsibility or duty.
5. Seeks privacy or aloneness.
6. Is autonomous or independent.
7. Repeatedly experiences the wonder of his/her life.
8. Frequently experiences awe or ecstacy and integrates the meaning into his/her life.
9. Experiences empathy or compassion for all human beings.
10. Has deep, though selective, interpersonal relationships with others.
11. Possesses democratic ideals.
12. Clearly distinguishes between means and ends.
13. Possesses a sense of humor devoid of hostility and sarcasm.
14. Creativeness.

Humanistic psychologists, therefore, focus on the loving, positive, creative and healthy. May (1969) eloquently states: "Care is a state in which something does _matter_; care is the opposite of apathy. Care is. . .the source of human tenderness. Fortunate, indeed, is it that care is born in the same act as the infant" (p. 289). The potential of man is unlimited from their prospectives.

If self-enhancing conditions are present, individuals will develop by allowing their selves to unfold and to grow.

Existentialism is a modern twentieth century philosophy which is often credited to Kierkegaard, a philosopher-psychologist-theologian. Much confusion exists in attempting to state an Existential philosophy for most Existentialists do not even choose to be labeled as such. Marler (1975) states that Existentialism as a philosophic system has been an influence in public education since the 1940's. This influence has been a protest focusing on a depersonalization of man in mass society. Heidigger, Neitzshe and Sartre generally are considered to be atheistic Existentialists while Kierkegaard, Tillich and Buber are thought of an theistic Existentialists. The Humanistic psychologists, Maslow, Fromm, May, Kelley, Combs and Rogers have attempted to translate Existential thought into education and counseling realities.

According to Morris (1961), the Existentialist believes that the ultimate questions of life cannot be fully answered with finality. However, trying to answer them is what life is all about. The Existentialist aim of education is first and foremost to understand oneself (Green, 1967). Basic tenets of Existentialism presented by Bates and Johnson (1972) may help the reader clarify Existential thought applied to the educational process.

1. Existence precedes essence.
   Human beings exist and must define themselves. Living is a process of self definition.

2. Man is condemned to freedom.
   Only when persons use their sentences of freedom to make conscious choices are they really alive. Each human must choose for him/herself and accept full responsibility for the consequences of those choices. Being aware of the implications of their freedom Existential

persons stand up to it as best they
can. "The non-Existentialist can
enjoy the security of being other
directed" (p. 22)

3. When man chooses, he chooses for all men.
As humans make choices they are aware
that they are the only representatives
of humankind, they have and, therefore,
inherent in choices are the implications
that this is best for every human.

4. Man defines himself only through his
actions.
Man defines himself only through what
he does, not by what he says he is going
to do nor what he intended to do. According to Existentialists the final rele-
vance is action. Feelings are relevant
and worth exploration only in understanding the barriers to action.

5. Two worlds exist--the world of objective
reality and the world of subjective
reality.
A world of objective reality exists and
is more or less knowable by scientific
laws to human beings. However, a world
of subjective reality governed by more
or less unknown psychological laws exists
and is only tentatively knowable by
human beings.

This brief discussion of Humanistic psychology
and Existential philosophy has been presented as
the roots of education for Design C.

The Language of Schooling

As persons seek to identify their philosophic
roots it is helpful to have a classification tool
for categorizing various opinions about schooling.
The model entitled, The Language of Schooling, is
presented as such a device. The content of the
model is presented for contemplation and discussion purposes only and is not intended to be final

in nature.

The model is an attempt to identify and contrast philosophical and psychological profiles that tend to separate into three camps: 1) Design A; 2) Design B; and 3) Design C. This separation is quite possibly a direct reflection of whether persons are primarily concerned with doing to, for, or with young people. The three camps can be dispersed on a continuum ranging from training to education.*

Training (To)   (For)   (With) Education

←———→

(Essentialism- (Experimentalism- (Existentialism-
  Behaviorism)   Cognitive)   Humanism)

An educational program committed to the training end of the continuum is based in the notion that human beings are the sum total of their experiences--passive victims of their environments. Conversely, the opposite end of the continuum is committed to the notion that human beings are active, goal-seeking organisms eager to profit from encounters with the environment.

The basic elements of the model, as they apply to each of the three profiles, are categorized into four parts: 1) philosophy; 2) psychology; 3) daily operations; and 4) definitions.

---

*For a more extensive discussion relative to this point the reader is referred to Chapter VI in Dobson and Dobson. Humaneness in the Schools: A Neglected Force, Dubuque, Iowa: Kendall/Hunt Publishers, 1976.

BASIC ELEMENTS	Design A Movement Toward External Control	Design B	Design C Movement Toward Internal Control

← ———————————————————————→

PHILOSOPHY

Human Nature	Humans are potentially evil.	Humans are potentially both good and bad or blank slate.	Humans are potentially good.
Nature of Learning	Truth exists separate from the individual. There are basic facts that are necessary for all. Learning occurs by reaction.	Truth is relative and subject to the condition of the learner and the environment. Learning occurs by action.	Truth is an individual matter. Learning occurs when the information encountered takes on personal meaning for the learner. Learning occurs by transaction and interaction.
Nature of Knowledge	Logical structure. Information. Subject matter. Vertical relationship. Universal.	Psychological structure. Vertical and horizontal. Relationships and interrelationships.	Perceptual structure. Relationships and Interrelationships. Personal. Gestalt.
Nature of Society	Closed. Ordered. Institutionalized. Static. Grouping. Con-	In flux. Democratic. Relative values. Experimentation.	Open, Self reviewing. Individual. Liberating. Distribution. Egalitarian.
Purpose of Education	To understand and apply knowledge. To control the environment. To learn absolute truth.	To learn prerequisite skills for survival. To learn conditional truths.	To live a full life. To experience the environment. To continue learning personal truth.

56

PSYCHOLOGY

Human Growth and Development	Growth is environment determined.	Gowth is the realization of one's potential.	Growth is the experiencing of one's potential.
Concept of Self	Determined by what others think. Focuses on personality deficiencies.	Determined by how the individual perceives the social environment (becoming-future orientation).	Determined and created by each individual (being-now orientation).
Human Emotions	Controlled. Closed. Unaware. Masked.	Circumstantial. Objective. Based on position. Well-adjusted.	Free. Openness. Spontaneity. Aware. Transparency. Experienced.
Interpersonal Interactions	Role Playing. Manipulative games. Defensive. Detached. Distrusting. Dependent.	Minimum Risk. Selective. Objective. Exclusive. Encountering. Independent.	Sharing. Risking. Trusting.

OPERATIONAL

Curriculum	Predetermined. Structured series. Logical sequence. Content centered. Outcomes established.	Sequenced experiences. Problem-centered. Future utility. Universalism.	Hidden. Unfolding. Created. Process centered. Unlimited. Emerging. Dynamic.
Instructional Behavior	Transmission of facts and content. Purposeful. Management. Teacher directed.	Grouping for instructional convenience. Inquiring. Discovering. Open questions with multiple answers. Teacher invitation.	Learner directed. Learner invitations. Teacher functions as source of safety and support.
Organization	Established. Emphasis on management. Focus on homogeneous grouping.	Orchestration. Focus on skill grouping.	Changing. Circumstantial. Adaptive. Focus on heterogeneous grouping.

| Evalua-tion | Measurement of facts and content. Determined by authority. Imposed. Product oriented. | Critical thinking. Problem solving. Tests higher cognitive skills. Focuses on what is learned. | Feedback by invitation. Cooperative pupil and teacher evaluation. Non-damaging comparison. Focuses on how one feels about what is learned as well as what is learned. |

DEFINITION

| Defini-tions of Curriculum | A structured series of intended learning outcomes.

- M. Johnson (1967) | A sequence of potential experiences set up in school for the purposes of disciplining children and youth in group ways of thinking and acting.

Smith, Stanley, Shores (1957) | An attempted definition of man translated into educational specifications.

- R. Dobson (1976) |

| Repre-senta-tive Language | Structure. Management. Reinforcement. Shaping. Labeling. Performance. Accountability. Objectives. Behavior. Matching. Environment. Cause-effect. Measurement. Observation. Transmission of roles. Function. Control. Intelligence. Reality. Order. Standards. Tests. Grades. Cover. Direct. | Sequence. Stages. Growth. and Development. Becoming. Correlated. Interest. Programs. Diagnostic. Readiness. Technique. Skills. Activity. Individual differences. Rational. Well-adjusted. Motivation. Progress. Expectations. Understanding. Discipline. Knowledge. Evaluation. Enable. Support. Facilitate. Guide. Help. Interests. Meaningful. | Being. Desires. Process. Democratic. Freedom. Feedback. Fulfillment. Experience. Diversity. Perception. Potential. Harmony. Personal order. Self-direction. Accepting. Unique. Consequences. Awareness. Sharing. Trusting. Allow. Experiment. Involve. Issues. Options. Natural. Spontaneous. Personal meaning. |

58

Philosophy

Human Nature

The philosophy of human nature possessed by persons influences how they interact with youngsters. Those who adhere to a Design A profile believe that the potential of human nature tends toward evil. Therefore, children must be directed and controlled. These educators attempt to shape learners according to adult values and teach children what they should know.

Inherent in Design B, a neutral belief of human nature, are expressions of restrained warmth as youngsters are maneuvered toward predetermined goals. These educators begin with children where they currently are functioning and manipulate the environment so that the children have the best possible experience based upon the adult's perception of what is best. These educators encourage the potential effectiveness of humanity by opening choice making, problem solving, creativity, and autonomy.

Design C persons believe that the potential of human nature is basically good; humans are cooperative and constantly seeking experiences that enhance their unique selves. These educators accept each child and provide stability as they interact with others in the school setting.

Nature of Learning

Design A educators adhere to mental faculty psychology and see the mind as a giant psychological storehouse capable of receiving and holding in cold storage a multitude of facts, concepts and skills. When the occasion calls for one or another of these particles of learning, the mind delivers it to the stage of action. Appropriate methods for the development of various skills include drill, practice, habit formation, and conditioning.

Theories of teaching-learning derived from

Design B focus on a blend of the teacher as a
manipulator and the intellectual structures that
characterize what is to be taught. This approach
concentrates on how children think and how their
thinking changes with age.

Design C educators see experiencing, being,
and learning as a totality that is dochotomized
only after the fact. Macdonald, Wolfson, and
Zaret (1973) establish: "Learning emerges in the
flow and continuity of man's total experiencing
and growing; growth is not a static process, nor
can there be static outcomes of learning" (p. 8).

Nature of Knowledge

Many people think of the school curriculum
as composed of highly separate subjects which
have very little relationship to each other. There
does not seem to be a clear distinction between
that which is information and that which is knowledge. We believe that information becomes knowledge only when it takes on personal meaning for
the individual.

The nature of knowledge encompasses many questions: how knowing takes place, how we know what
we know, how we decide what knowledge is most
worth having, and how we know reality. Answers
to these questions are arrived at differently for
those subscribing to either Design A, Design B,
or Design C.

Proponents of Design A submit the existence
of a central body of knowledge that must be transmitted to all. This truth is pre-existent to the
learning of it. The most valid way of discovering
truth is the empirical method (sense experience).
The test of truth is its correspondence to reality.

Design B advocates assert that knowledge is
rooted in experience. Individuals "create" knowledge as they interact with the total environment.
Knowledge is therefore tentative. As individuals
grow, develop and change, knowledge of what is true

will also change. Information becomes knowledge when it is considered relevant to the solution of a particular problem.

Design C educators submit that persons can be certain of only that which can be experienced, streams of thoughts and feelings. They are in concert with Design B proponents when they establish that truth cannot be settled once and for all because the individual is constantly becoming, that is, constantly making choices and changing .

Nature of Society

When a society begins to fear its culture is not important to the young then education must be made to happen. The degree to which the school should seek to reflect or reconstruct the society becomes an issue of debate.

According to Design A, school is one of the most important institutions in society whose purpose is preservation of the culture. In other words the school is the tool for maintaining existing social orders when the public has decided on them; however, school does not create them. The task becomes one of developing a standardized student-citizen as the product of the system .

Conversely, for Design B educators, society is a process in which individuals participate. The major role of the school is to teach the adults of the future to deal with the planning necessarily involved in the process called society. Education must serve as a source of new ideas.

Design C advocates believe that the way to improve society is through improving the quality of individuals, not through improving institutions. The school's primary task is individual; that is, the school should concentrate upon the development of absolute freedom in the child. The tendency is toward an egalitarian society.

Purpose of Education

The time seems to be appropriate for people from the three basic camps to declare what they see as the purpose of education. Clark and Beatty (1967) ask the question:

Do we shape learners according to our values and teach them what they should know? Or, do we foster the potential effectiveness of humanity by open choice making, problem solving, creativity, and autonomy and follow the results where-ever they may go? (p. 70)

This is a question that seldom is asked in educational circles, let alone discussed with any personal intentions. The manner with which persons respond to this question probably places them in one or another of the three camps.

If persons view the purpose of education as one of transmitting to the young universal truth, then they are definitely aligned with Design A. If they view truth as relative and subject to time, circumstance, and place and the task of the school as teaching survival skills to the young, then they can probably be classified as Design B proponents. However, if persons view truth as a personal matter to be established by individuals as they experience their potentials then they are advocates of Design C.

Psychology

Human Growth and Development

The definition of human growth is crucial to formulating a dialogue relative to schooling. Growth as defined by those advocating Design A results in a disease or pathological model. That is, educators' behaviors resemble that of the medical profession as they focus on deficiencies of youngsters by diagnosing, prescribing, and treating.

If Design A subscribes to a medical model,

then Design B subscribes to an agronomy model. Children are seen as passing through various developmental stages as they move toward realization of potential. Just as a stalk of corn grows toward maturity and must receive the proper care, so it is with young children as they move toward their potentials. The value of current experiences are assessed by their future value.

Design C advocates define growth as the experiencing of one's potential. The present is stressed for it's own value. Children are not viewed as miniature or pre-adults. Potential is not something one prepares for, but rather is something one already is.

Concept of Self

If growth is seen as environmentally determined, then self concept is determined by what others think and focuses on personality deficiencies. This is the belief of Design A advocates.

Since Design B educators view potential as something to be realized, they purport that self concept is determined by how the individual receives and interprets feedback from the environment. The emphasis is on becoming and, therefore, Design B proponents have a future orientation.

In contrast, Design C educators establish that a concept of self is an extension and expression of self as each experiences his/her potential. The emphasis is on being and, therefore, Design C proponents have a "now" orientation.

Human Emotions and Interpersonal Interactions

Design A educators, since they are victims of their environment, see relationships ". . .as having two alternatives: to control or be controlled" (Shostrom, 1968, p. 24). Therefore, they tend to play roles, maneuver and conceal motives in interactions with others. Persons of this belief tend to be possessive and quite dependent.

Well-adjusted may be a term that best describes ideal human emotions and interpersonal interactions from the Design B perspective. Therefore, these advocates are intent upon programming children toward conformity and adjustment to society and its institutions. Minimum risk and selectivity in interpersonal interactions are quite descriptive of Design B proponent.

Emotions of Design C educators are spontaneously and freely expressed; they have the freedom and courage to be, to express their potentials. Self-fulfillment rather than adjustment is a key difference. These persons honestly express their feelings in authentic relationships and communicate nonpossessiveness in their involvement with others.

Operational

Curriculum

Curriculum, according to Design A, is predetermined and results in subject matter that is highly structured and logical. Curriculum is definitely content centered.

The curriculum, according to Design B, results in the sequencing of learning experiences that are problem-centered. Future utility and universalism are givens as far as selection of content is concerned. The sequencing of content is based on identified stages of development.

In Design C, spontaneous interaction has the potential for unfolding and allowing to surface and to emerge an unlimited source of curriculum that is dynamic and emerges as a consequence of the students' needs, wants, and desires.

Instructional Behavior

The instructional behavior of Design A teachers is reflective of their philosophy of human nature and their beliefs about the purposes of education. As a consequence of these beliefs they attempt to indoctrinate. The transmisson of verifiable facts is paramount. Instructional activities are pre-planned with specific performance objectives clearly stated.

Design B teachers often use questioning as an instructional strategy. Questions are open and multiple answers are sought for discussion purposes. Grouping is seen as the way for individualizing instruction.

The instructional behavior of the teacher who adheres to Design C is determined by the learner and occurs only by invitation from the learner. The teacher does not impose nor trespass into the learner's personal space until an invitation has been extended.

Organization

Organizational arrangement according to Design A is rigid and orderly in nature; emphasis is on management and efficiency. As a consequence of the organizational design being established, time-space becomes segmented. Thus, subject-matter is segregated and parceled according to time allotments.

The organization of school, by Design B, is an orchestrated expression of the curriculum and instructional arrangement. Subject matter assumes universalism and focuses on utility. Flexible scheduling is related to instructional needs of the staff, not the students. Individualized instruction occurs by pacing the learner through study sequences.

In Design C, organization is adaptive to the circumstances that occur as a consequence of time-space blend. Individual learners plan their own use of time within limits of personal and social order.

Evaluation

Evaluation in Design A is based on comparisons and is product oriented. The measurement of facts and content is imperative in the evaluation of student learning. Evaluation standards and procedures are determined by authority and these, in turn, are imposed upon students.

Design B attempts to evaluate critical thinking, problem solving, and higher cognitive skills. This approach focuses on what is learned and attempts to utilize this information in prescribing future learning tasks.

Evaluation, by Design C, is solicited from the learner and the norm is self-established. Feedback is available upon request and is a shared experience, as opposed to being imposed from without.

Definition

Differing assumptions concerning school functions, what should be taught and how learning should occur, result in at least three varying yet basic definitions of curriculum. These three basic definitions of curriculum are presented in the model. Each of the definitions reflect a different perspective relative to the purpose of school. The definition selected determines the complexion of the educative process provided for youngsters.

A Concluding Comment

Despite certain limitations, our model enables the reader to make useful distinctions among educational directions proposed by three basic groups. It is probably safe to say that these directions are seldom, if ever, found in pure form; however, most schools are patterned after one of the three.

This chapter makes no attempt to provide answers to questions about what schools should teach or how any curriculum should be organized. In a sense, the model is analytical. We hope that readers will find the categorizations of the model useful for organizing their thoughts concerning the goals, content, and organization of any school as they seek to interact with persons in a constructive manner.

SUMMARY

1. The purposes of schooling have become obscure.

2. Deciding on the purposes of schooling require responses to complex questions for which there are probably no best answers.

3. Words used to discuss the purposes of schooling have become blurred by custom and usage.

4. There is need for a tool for dialogue to assist educators in approaching the complex questions of schooling with some degree of clarity.

5. In creating a model for schooling dialogue, one approach is to categorize school functions according to the philosophic base they reflect.

6. Division has sharpened among three distinct educational camps: behaviorism, experimentalism, and humanism.

7. These three distinct camps have resulted in different definitions of curriculum each of which dictates different perspectives and approaches to the schooling process.

8. Schools are seldom, if ever, established in pure form; however, most schools are patterned after one of the three identified approaches.

REFERENCES

Bates, Marilyn M. and Johnson, C. D. Group leadership. Denver, Colorado: Love Publishing Company, 1972.

Bigge, M. L. Learning theories for teachers. New York: Harper and Row Publishers, 1964.

Bruner, J. S. The process of education. Cambridge: Harvard University Press, 1960.

Bruner, J. S. Contemporary approaches to cognition. Cambridge: Harvard University Press, 1957.

Bruner, J. S., Goodnow, J. J., Austin, G. A. A study of thinking. New York: Wiley, 1957.

Clark, R. J., Beatty, W. H. Learning and evaluation. In T. Wilhelms (Ed.), Evaluation as feedback and guide. Washington, D.C.: Association of Supervision and Curriculum Development, 1967.

Combs, A. W. and Snygg, D. Individual behavior. New York: Harper and Row, 1959.

Dawson, R. G. A conceptual framework to assess the degree of philosophical harmony within the elementary school. Unpublished Doctoral Dissertation. Stillwater, Oklahoma: Oklahoma State University, 1976.

Dewey, J. Experience and education. Toronto, Ontario: Collier-Macmillan Canada Ltd. 1963. Copyright, Kappa Delta Pi, 1938.

Dimick, K. M. and Huff, V. E. Child counseling. Dubuque, Iowa: Wm. C. Brown, 1970.

Dobson, R. L. and Dobson, Judith E. Humaneness in schools: A neglected force. Dubuque, Iowa: Kendall/Hunt Publishers, 1976.

Ebel, R. L. What are schools for? Phi Delta Kappan, 1972, 14, 3-7.

Eisner, E. The curriculum field today: Where we are, where we were. Unpublished paper read at the Society of Professors of Curriculum. Houston: March, 1977.

Frazier, A. Here and now: Points of decision in the quest for a new curriculum. In R. Leeper (Ed.), A man for tomorrow's world. Washington, D.C.: Association of Supervision and Curriculum Development, 1970.

Gasset, Jose, Ortega Y. The origin of philosophy, Translated by T. Talbot. New York: W.W. Norton and Company, Inc., 1967.

Gobel, F. The third force. New York: Grossman Publishers, 1970.

Goldenson, R. M. The encyclopedia of human behavior. New York: Dell Publishing Company, 1975.

Green, Maxine. Existential encounters for teachers. New York: Random House, 1967.

Johnson, M. Definitions and models in curriculum theory. Educational Theory, 1967, 17, 127-31.

Jourard, S. The transparent self. New York: Reinhard, Van Nostrand, 1964.

Kneller, J. F. Existentialism and education. New York: Philosophical Library, Inc., 1964.

Marler, C. D. Philosophy and schools. Boston: Allyn and Bacon, Inc., 1975.

Marshall, J. P. The teacher and his philosophy. Lincoln, Nebraska: Professional Educators Publications, Inc., 1973.

Maslow, A. H. Motivation and personality, 2nd ed., New York: Harper and Row, 1959.

Maslow, A. H. Self-actualizing people: A study of psychological health. In C.E. Moustakas (Ed.), The self: Explorations in personal growth. New York: Harper and Row, 1956.

May, R. Love and will. New York: W.W. Norton and Company, Inc., 1969.

Macdonald, J., Wolfson, B., Zaret, Esther. Re-schooling society: A conceptual model. Washington, D.C.: Association of Supervision and Curriculum Development, 1973.

Morris, V. C. Philosophy and the American school. Boston: Houghton Mifflin Company, 1961.

Myers, D. The humanistic school--A definition. Forum on Open Education, 1976, 4, 3-7.

Patterson, C. H. Humanistic education. Englewood Cliffs, New Jersey: Prentice-Hall, Inc., 1973.

Piaget, J. The psychology of the child. Translated by Helen Weaver. New York: Basic Books, 1969.

Rogers, C. R. On personal power. New York: Dela-corte Press, 1977.

Rogers, C. R. On becoming a person. Boston: Houghton Mifflin, 1961.

Rogers, C. R. The necessary and sufficient conditions of therapeutic personality change. Journal of Consulting Psychology, 1957, 21, 95-103.

Sargent, S. S., Stafford, K. R. Basic teachings of the great psychologists. Garden City, New York: Doubleday and Company, Inc., 1965.

70

Shostrom, E. Man, the manipulator. New York: Bantam Books, 1968.

Smith, B. O., Stanley, W., and Shores, J. Fundamentals of curriculum. New York: Harcourt, Brace and World, Inc., 1957.

Sulzer, Beth and Mayer, G. R. Behavior modification procedures for school personnel. Hinsdale, Illinois: The Dryden Press, Inc., 1972.

Thorndike, E. L. Selected writings from a connectionist's psychology. New York: Appleton-Century-Crofts, 1949.

Thorndike, E. L. Educational psychology. New York: Teachers College, Columbia University, 1913.

Thorndike, E. L. Education. New York: Macmillan, 1912.

Wadsworth, B. J. Piaget's theory of cognitive development. New York: David McKay Company, Inc., 1971.

Wingo, G. M. Philosophies of education: An introduction. Lexington, Massachusetts: D.C. Heath and Company, 1974.

CHAPTER IV

THE PERSON OF THE TEACHER

We have dealt extensively about our belief that the person should be central to the professional role of teacher. We have affirmed our belief that the person of the teacher should not be assigned the position of spectator in the affairs of schooling, but rather should assume a posture of active involvement.

But what is this person of the teacher we have discussed? Can the person of a role fit into and contribute to the goals of an institution that has a bureaucratic base? We think so.

This chapter will attempt to explore the person of the teacher. From our perspective, any revolution in education will necessarily involve introducing the unique person of the teacher into the classroom. With the uniqueness of each individual teacher prized in the schools then and only then will the uniqueness of individual children also be emphasized. When this emphasis upon the uniqueness of individual persons in the schools is achieved then learning, total personal development, will flourish. Teachers and children are first of all persons: persons are far more than a description of their role behaviors.

The main thesis of this book has emphasized that schools are complex social organizations and that simplistic approaches to improving the quality of schools are ineffective. Furthermore, social organizations are composed of individual persons. In order to improve the quality of schools, emphasis must be placed upon the individuals who interact together daily. West (1972) states that schools have sanctioned an organizational farce by assuming that all teachers are alike in needs, abilities and aspirations: a teacher is not ". . . a carbon copy of his colleagues" (p. 249). He continues that because schools tend to view teachers as if they were cast from the same mold, many experience loss of identity and alienation from self. This results in the schools benefiting neither the students nor the teachers.

Personal Philosophy

Individuals possess a philosophy of life whether or not they are cognizant of it. One's philosophy, personal values and beliefs, form the foundation from which one makes choices or decisions during his/her lifetime. Broadly speaking, one's philosophy is a personal system of principles for living one's life.

Beliefs

Basic to a teacher's personal philosophy is his/her belief in human nature or the belief about people and how they grow and develop. Combs', et.al. (1969) research in the helping professions (teaching being one of these) concludes that the system of beliefs that helpers hold of others is an extremely important variable in their effectiveness. They continue that beliefs enable helpers to be spontaneous in their transactions with others. Purkey and Avila (1971) also emphasize that the teacher's beliefs concerning the worth and dignity of individuals is paramount and that in order to identify good and poor teachers it is necessary to explore how teachers see themselves and the world around them.

Traditionally, the major thrust in teacher effectiveness research has been an emphasis on the teaching-learning process. Basically, this research includes studies concerned with various instructional methodologies and pupil achievement (Russell and Fea, 1963; Good, Biddle and Brophy, 1975; Fisher, Mariave and Filby, 1979), teacher characteristics and teaching effectiveness (Getzels and Jackson, 1963; Raskow, Airasian and Madaus, 1978), and teache

74

behaviors as related to pupil achievement (Withall and Lewis, 1963; Rosenshine, 1976; Good, 1979).

However, research in the area of teacher effectiveness has been unable to demonstrate that effectiveness is strictly a function of scholarship, certain personality traits, or that there are good or bad methods apart from the persons and purposes involved (Combs, 1965). According to Biddle and Ellena (1964) the problem of teacher effectiveness is so complex that to delineate just what the competent teacher is becomes difficult.

A further review of research and literature in the field of education reveals an equal concern for the humanizing factor in the educational process. Humanistic inquiries center around teacher expectancy studies (Rosenthal and Jacobson, 1968, Davidson and Lang, 1960), interpersonal relationship studies (Rogers, 1962; Combs, 1970) and learning climate studies (Anderson and Walberg, 1967; Sinclair, 1968; Dobson, Grey and Dobson, 1979).

School systems are, in many ways, developed and maintained by teachers and principals. These are the personnel who establish and maintain the physical, social and psychological environments which possibly affect, in some manner, the academic, social and emotional performance or growth of students (Davidson and Lang, 1960). Certainly, it is within the school and classroom systems that teachers and pupils act, react, interact, and possibly transact. It is also here that effective teacher leadership along with environmental conditions become of collective, interactive importance in developing a climate conducive to fostering desirable growth.

According to Beniskos (1971), "Teaching is not just a matter of possessing skills, nor of being possessed by skills either" (p. 35). He continues that it is too easy to hide behind skills and thus avoid relating to people. Beniskos emphasizes that skills are those things which a teacher adds to what he/she already is. Usher and Hanke (1971) agree when they state:

The primary "tool" with which teachers
work is themselves. Effective teaching
is thus seen as effective use of the
teacher's own self; the peculiar ways
in which he is able to combine his own
knowledge and sensitivity with his own
unique ways of putting it into operation
so as to be helpful to others (p. 3).

Therefore, Usher and Hanke (1971) recommend
that educators attempt understanding the effective
teacher from a "self as instrument" approach (p. 3).
They contend that teachers, like everyone else, are
unique individuals. The "self as instrument" concept concerning teaching means that teacher effectiveness is a personal matter of the effective use
of a unique self. This particular orientation helps
to account for why attempts to determine teacher
effectiveness as a result of knowledge, personality
traits, competencies and methods have not proved
fruitful. The search for common characteristics and
knowledge disregards the individuality of the teachers themselves. Usher and Hanke emphasize that the
nature and quality of teachers' personal beliefs
become crucial; teachers convey their beliefs through
their methods, knowledge and procedures or in spite
of specific procedures used in the classroom. Sanders
and Sanders (1978) very succinctly state that the
"person" of the teacher is the most important factor
in the learning process.

Goodlad (1977) echoes this sentiment and calls
upon teachers to examine beliefs and to act respon-
sibly so that they do not violate their own integrity.
Seaberg (1974) also emphasizes that it is necessary
for a teacher to clarify his/her beliefs about people
and how they learn if he/she is to facilitate growth.
She continues that teachers must not be ambivalent
in their beliefs.

Since teachers play a significant part in determining the educational environment, it is important
to have some expectations about the nature of their
behavior. Wrightsman (1964) states that the importance of these expectations or assumptions about

76

what people are really like influence our interactions with others. Combs (1962) further emphasizes the importance of a person's basic beliefs
about human nature and the influence of this phenomenon upon human interactions in the educational
process.

The nature of humans relative to good and
evil is expressed in many ways. Durant (1953) contends that to be good does not merely mean to be
obedient and harmless. He continues that goodness
without ability is lame and that virture alone will
not save one if he/she lacks intelligence.

Spinoza's (1952) interpretation of human nature
emphasizes that humans are in a constant state of
change and moving toward a particular model. He
states:

> With regard to good and evil, these terms
> indicate nothing positive in things con-
> sidered in themselves, nor are they any-
> thing else than modes of thought, or
> notions which we form from the comparison
> of one thing with another. For one and
> the same thing may at the same time be
> both good and evil or indifferent. But
> although things are so we must retain
> these words. For since we desire to
> form for ourselves an idea of man upon
> which we may look as a model of human na-
> ture, it will be of service to us to re-
> tain these expressions in the sense I
> have mentioned (p. 423).

According to Dewey (1910), human nature is
good. He believed, as did Spinoza, that humans
are in a state of change and that goodness resides
within them.

The concept of human nature extends into the
interactions within the classroom. Kelley and
Rasey (1952) point out that the teacher's basic
beliefs about human nature help to define the relationship with students. Essentially, all teachers
have experienced teacher education curricula which

have great similarity, yet teaching behavior and learning climates from classroom to classroom seem to possess a high degree of variability (Ragan, 1953). What might affect these differences is a research question of great magnitude. There is a need to critique the research literature relative to a teacher's philosophy of human nature and the academic, social, and psychological growth of children.

Most people have definite beliefs about human nature and frequently use these basic assumptions to explain and describe the actions of others. The phrase, "it is human nature to do this . . . or that," can be heard almost daily. Although people continually refer to the manner in which others act and react in terms of their assumptions about human nature, attempts to quantify and measure this pervasive concept have been scarce. More recently, however, social scientists have come to realize that people's assumptions about human nature can be conceptualized and measured, and one can determine if these beliefs influence behavior toward others.

Dobson, Sewell and Shelton (1974) investigated the relationship between teachers' views of human nature and the congruence of their verbal and nonverbal behavior in the classroom. Each teacher was observed for 20 minutes by two trained observers on two separate occasions. They found no significant difference between the overall positive or negative philosophy of human nature possessed by teachers and the congruence of verbal-nonverbal behavior. However, there was a change in the congruence of verbal-nonverbal behavior of the two groups on the last observation. Of the teachers holding a positive view of human nature, 70 percent were more congruent on the last observation than they were on the first. Of the teachers holding a negative view of human nature, 60 percent were less congruent on the last observation than they were on the first. They recommend additional observations in future research on the basis that a teacher may mask feelings for brief periods, but over an extended period of time nonverbal leakages will betray true feelings.

Childress and Dobson (1973) attempted to analyze the relationship between teachers' basic beliefs of human nature and students' perceptions of the educational environment. Although none of the relationships were statistically significant, the students' scores on the perceived environmental instrument were consistently higher for the teacher group expressing positive views of human nature.

Dobson, Hopkins, and Elsom (1973) sought to determine if the philosophy of human nature held by teachers is related to the nonverbal communication patterns of teachers and their pupils in the classroom setting. Significant differences were found. Teachers with a positive view of human nature tended to rank higher on the frequency of their nonverbal communication in the classroom. If a teacher believes that human nature is basically evil or neither good nor bad, then he/she will interact differently with others than the teacher who views human nature as basically good. The teacher viewing human nature as basically evil sees people as basically controlled by unconscious drives, as reactors and, therefore, not free (Seaberg, 1974). The teacher viewing others as neither good nor bad but neutral assumes the responsibility of programming children toward what "good" children should be or should do (Dobson and Dobson, 1976). However, the teacher viewing human nature as basically good sees people as having control over their lives, as proacters on their environments. People are viewed as capable of making choices that are consistent with their fellow human beings.

Inherent in teachers' beliefs concerning human nature are the concomitant beliefs, concerning the nature of learning, the nature of society and the purpose of education. Readers are encouraged to explore their belief systems by completing for themselves and discussion with others the following:

Human nature is . . .

Truth is . . .

Learning occurs by . . .

79

Knowledge is . . .

Society is . . .

The purpose of education is to . . .

The relationship between teacher's philosophies of human nature and selected educational variables seems to be an area of research worthy of expanded analysis. The following are pertinent questions which could be answered through additional research:

1. Is there a difference between the academic achievement of students whose teachers have a positive view of human nature?

2. Do variables such as age, sex, level of educational attainment and years of teaching experience relate to positive and negative values of human nature?

3. Is there a relationship between teachers' beliefs of human nature and their pupils' self-concept?

4. Is there a relationship between teachers' philosophies of human nature, their peer relationships and perceived classroom climate?

5. Is there a relationship between teachers' and principals' philosophies of human nature and the perceived school climate?

Hopefully, educational researchers will begin to focus on teachers' philosophies of human nature as a crucial area of study. This complex area of teacher beliefs holds many implications for classroom interactions that either hinder or facilitate the growth of children. Additional research is needed to identify these variables and their interrelations.

Values

Kemp (1967) stresses that technical thinking and planning have negatively influenced the sense

of community once prevalent in our society . He
states that there has occurred a depersonalization
in all forms of relationship in home, school, office
and factory. As a result, a person's values often
are second-hand introjections from many, often conflicting sources. There is a definite need for
teachers to recognize their own basic value structures and the value base of those with whom they
interact.

According to Katz and Stotland (1959) values
are a highly integrated set of attitudes about particular objects in an individual's environment.
One's values are generally lasting and deep seated
beliefs. Today, educators realize that value-neutrality on the part of the teacher is an impossibility. If teachers cannot maintain neutrality,
then they must be aware of the values they ex-
pouse.

Moustakas (1967) discusses what he terms universal values and self values. He defines universal values as ". . . values which have remained
essential throughout human history, giving the
individual and human life a whole meaning" (p. 2).
In terms of human relationships he emphasizes the
following universal values; honesty, love, beauty,
justice, truth and freedom. May (1953) states that
man's loneliness and anxiety result from a loss of
values that can be replaced only through overthrow-
ing psychological hangups that have created depend-
ence and through exercising the freedom to choose
one's self.

Self-values, according to Moustakas (1967),
are the resources existing within self; the interests, meanings and desires unique to each individual. He continues:

Self-values are in jeopardy in any climate
where freedom and choice are denied, in
any situation where the individual rejects
his own senses and substitutes for his own
perceptions the standards and exceptions
of others (p. 5} .

Values are an important element in an individual's life. And yet, many schools do not provide the freedom nor encourage individuals (teachers and students) to express and live by their own values. Students are often viewed not as total human beings but as producers and are judged on the number of correct answers or assignments completed. Competition rather than cooperation also is stressed based upon the notion that it's a hard, cruel world and teachers must prepare children and youth to compete in a dog-eat-dog society. Those students who "buy into" the values permeating many school systems are judged as winners; those who do not are evaluated as losers.

Likewise, teachers are often forced to accept or at least to play a role that they accept the values of a particular school system in order to keep their jobs. For example, schools prize intellectual values and some school systems still demand that grading be consistent with the normal curve. Therefore, if a teacher gives 2 A grades, he/she must then also give 2 F grades and so forth. Another value permeating some school systems (although not readily accepted by all teachers) is that learning is taking place only when the classroom is quiet.

Therefore, students and teachers alike may be engaging in self-betrayal of values (Moustakas, 1967) and forcing themselves to fit into another's plans and to interact with others in ways that have no personal meaning or value. Gordon (1974) states: "Teachers are members of an organization whose norms, rules, policies, prohibition, and job definitions strongly influence how they respond to students and how they teach them" (p. 307). In discussing values, Gordon (1974) comments that value conflicts or value collisions are likely to occur and that they cannot be avoided nor wished away. He mentions such values as drug use, proper language, honesty, justice, choice of friends, sexual behavior, manners, patriotism, religion, and personal grooming as frequent areas of value collisions in the schools. Gordon continues that one of the best ways to deal with value collisions is for the teacher to model the behavior he/she would like to establish. Gordon states:

> If you value honesty, then be honest with students. If you value neatness, then be neat in dress and manner. If you value promptness, be on time. If you value democratic principles, then don't be autocratic. But if you value fascism or the law of survival of the strongest, then don't try to preach democracy or humanitarianism (p. 299).

However, one of the greatest obstacles to teachers becoming models is the "double standard" prevailing in most school: Do as I say, not as I do. Therefore, Gordon suggests that dialogue between and among teachers, students and administrators is necessary in allowing all concerned to express and explore their values.

Since teachers expose their values in interaction with others and since value collisions are inherent in a pluralistic society, then the time has come to provide means for challenging teachers toward values/behavior congruency. Our society has expressed the value of the necessity of enlightened and knowledgeable populations through the establishment of a public school system. However, within the schools, intellectual values are stressed almost to the exclusion of social and human values. For example, a child may often be viewed in terms of his/her I.Q. score, achievement test scores and grades. Social values also are evident in school through extracurricular offerings. However, many of the clubs and teams do not create a sense of community but stress competition rather than cooperation, i.e. state music contests, science fairs and sports. Being "Number 1" is valued, not just being. Therefore, human values, the expression of the dignity and worth of each human in all his/her uniqueness, are often overlooked within schools.

Kelley (1962) states that the fully functioning individual, one who holds human values and
lives in keeping with his/her values, is motivated
toward the unfolding of self and others. Does the
school encourage fully functioning people? Does
the school encourage both teachers and students
to be themselves? Are teachers and students valued
for their individuality and autonomy? Is independence sought? Is personal meaning prized over
accumulation and reiteration of facts?

Questions such as these point out the human
dilemma that exists in schools as well as other
bureaucracies. The human dilemma is: How can a
person (teacher, student) express and maintain self
in a social environment (school) that demands
accommodation to an established norm?

We believe that by prizing the individuality
or the uniqueness of teachers, then the learning
environment of the school will become one of encouraging individuality of students. Sanders and
Sanders (1978) describe a learning environment as
one that: 1) respects, emphasizes and appreciates
the worth of each child; 2) encourages open communication and expression of feelings; and 3) encourages the discovering of understanding and knowledge. Therefore, they propose that learning
environments prize human values, social values
and intellectual values. By freeing the teacher
from playing the role of teacher, by encouraging
the person of the teacher to interact with others,
then such a learning environment is possible in
all schools.

Personal Sensitivity

The personal sensitivity of teachers, awareness of attitudes and feelings they experience
from moment to moment as well as the awareness
of the attitudes and feelings children are experiencing, is a tremendous influence in the classroom. What the teacher is experiencing at the
moment of interaction with a child will influence
his/her tone of voice, rate of speech, facial

expressions, gestures as well as verbal content. What the child is experiencing at the time of the interaction will definitely influence his/her acceptance of the teacher's message and the response. Therefore, attention must be paid to the sensitivity of the teacher, not only because it influences the communication processes within the classroom but because sensitivity or lack of sensitivity to self and others influences one's personal growth. Carkhuff and Berenson (1967) state ". . . the levels at which an individual functions with others reflect the levels of his attitudes and comprehension of himself . . ." (p. 26). Therefore, if teachers are encouraged to become aware of the sensitivity they express to others in the school, they must be provided means of exploring their own attitudes and feelings toward self.

Feelings

The word feelings may be one of the most overworked words in our vocabulary: it is used to express human conditions ranging from physical to emotional. Dobson, Dobson & Grahlman (1979) state: "Teachers talk about feelings, educational professors profess about them; psychologists research them; and all of us experience them" (p. 47).

We contend that the feelings experienced in a classroom whether they be positive (happiness, excitement, acceptance) or negative (anger, frustration, rejection) not only influence personal and social growth but also the academic growth of students. Leonard (1972) suggests that certain social conditions encourage the ignoring of emotions and the distrusting of one's own feelings. All too often parents and teachers will comment to a child: "Don't be angry with Jane, she's your friend;" or "Little boys don't cry." Therefore, children are told in many ways that what they are feeling is wrong. Is it no wonder that children learn not to tune into their own feelings, becoming less sensitive to their own emotions?

Dahms (1972) reinforces this view by suggesting

85

that people are taught to suppress and control feelings rather than to express them. He states that interpersonal relationships occur, more often than not, at an intellectual level (playing a role, wearing a facade) as opposed to an emotional level (mutual accessibility, openness). The result is superficial contact between and among humans. He presents an argument for emotional intimacy as a basic requirement for true human survival.

Moustakas (1967) seems to define an emotionally intimate relationship in the classroom:

> Relations must be such that the child is free to recognize, actualize, and experience his own uniqueness. Teachers help to make this possible when they show they deeply care for the child, respect his individuality, and accept the child's being without qualifications. To permit the child to be and become is not to promote selfishness, but to affirm his truly human self (p. 33).

Hamachek (1969) related that good teachers view teaching as primarily a human process involving human relationships and human meanings. He continues that flexibility and the ability to perceive the world from the student's point of view (both influence human relationships) seem to distinguish the more effective from the less effective teacher. Combs' (1965) points out that good teachers feel adequate rather than untrustworthy, wanted rather than unwanted, worthy rather than unworthy and feel an identification with people as opposed to feeling alienated or apart from others.

Personal Psychological Structure

How teachers feel about themselves, their psychological postures, definitely influence what happens or what does not happen in the classroom. The fears or insecurities some teachers possess concerning their own personal worth may create barriers to honest personal encounters with youngsters (Dobson and Dobson, 1976). The work

of Usher and Hanke (1971) and Sanders and Sanders
(1978) have been mentioned previously in this chapter. However, when speaking of the teacher's psychological posture, a reiteration of the "self as
instrument" (Usher and Hanke, 1971) to understanding effective teaching is necessary. This concept
concerning teaching emphasizes that teacher effectiveness is a personal matter of the effective use
of a unique self. Sanders and Sanders (1978) propose that the most important factor in the learning
process is the person of the teacher. The following discussion will focus on self concept, personality characteristics, self-fulfilling prophecies
and needs.

Self Concept

Self esteem, self concept and self image are
terms that are discussed at length by educators.
Books and articles are written on the topic and
educators attempt to measure it through standardized inventories and make inferences about it
through observation. Most educators will argue
that self concept, the image a person holds of
self, is not objective and does influence thoughts,
perceptions and behaviors. The developmental aspect of self concept has been described by many
researchers (Allport, 1937; Engel, 1959; Purkey,
1970; and Wyne, White and Coop, 1974).

The self concepts of teachers are continuously
influenced by those who interact with them as responsible and valuable or those who interact with
them as irresponsible and unable. Purkey (1978,
p. 30) states "one's self-concept is a complex,
continuously active system of subjective beliefs
about one's personal existence." The self concept
serves as a guide or a reference point for one's
behavior (Glock, 1972). Therefore, all that a
person experiences is filtered through and mediated
by his/her self concept, an image one has learned
from significant others over the years. Since one's
perceptions of self are learned over a period of
time, they are quite resistant to change (Purkey,
1978). If the self concept serves as a guide and
mediator of perceptions, thoughts and actions then

the image a teacher has of self is of utmost importance. Combs (1965) speaks eloquently to this
topic.

Beniskos (1971) proposed that the teacher
should be aware of his/her (1) greatness, (2) uniqueness, (3) need to love and be loved, and (4) potential to develop fully. He stresses that if teachers
feel great, they are also aware that greatness
applies to everyone and, therefore, respect and
communication are facilitated. Likewise, if teachers
recognize their uniqueness, then they will respect
the fact that each child is also unique. Beniskos
emphasizes that once teachers realize their need to
love and be loved, then they can accept the same in
a child. "Once a teacher loves, he grow, and the
children grow" (Beniskos, 1971, p. 36). He also
suggests that by viewing self as a developing human
being, teachers encourage the personal development
of individual children.

Hamachek (1969) and Deiken and Fox (1973) suggest that if it is true that good teachers have a
positive view of themselves and others, then more
opportunities should be provided for both preservice
and inservice teachers to acquire more positive
self perceptions. Jersild (1955) has demonstrated
that when "teachers face themselves," they feel
more adequate as individuals and function more
effectively as teachers.

Personality Characteristics

Many research efforts aimed at investigating
teacher effectiveness have attempted to delineate
personal characteristics of good versus poor teacher.
deBruin (1969) suggests ". . . that so-called good
teachers, at any level, do not fit into any 'common
mold'" (p. 241). He stresses that the effectiveness
of the teaching act is an individual matter involving aspects of a teacher's personality. He continues that effective teaching seems to involve persons' insights into their own capabilities and
limitations. How teachers think others perceive
them and how they perceive themselves are important

clues to predicting effective classroom performance.

Both deBruin (1969) and Usher and Hanke (1971) stress the need for learning to use self as an effective instrument in the classroom. The effective teacher is original in his/her performance, creative in his/her thinking and flexible in adjusting to the learning situation. Therefore, the good teacher possesses versatility, flexibility and creativity.

deBruin's (1969) research indicates that students were able to correlate good teaching with the following ten aspects of personaltiy. Good teachers 1) show good perception and knowledge of subject matter; 2) are sensitive to the needs of individual students; 3) believe that students want to learn and have the ability to learn the material being presented; 4) feel that students respect him/her as an individual; 5) display complete faith and trust in students; 6) are enthusiastic about teaching; 7) radiate an air of self-confidence; 8) perform as a helper rather than a dictator in the classroom; 9) use teaching techniques suited to their individual personalities; and 10) show evidence of having happy home lives.

Powell (1978) emphasizes that teachers can and do make a difference in how students learn. She continues that "teachers cannot rely upon one method of teaching or one set of teaching behaviors to be effective in all teaching situations" (p. 30).

After a review of literature, Hamachek (1969) states that effective teachers appear to be those who are human in the fullest sense. They have a sense of humor, are fair, empathetic, more democratic than autocratic, and are able to relate easily and naturally to students on either a one-to-one or group basis. The classrooms of effective teachers seem to reflect an openness, spontaneity and adaptability to change. In contrast, ineffective teachers apparently lack a sense of humor, grow impatient easily, use ego-reducing comments in class, are less well integrated, are inclined to be somewhat authoritarian and are generally less sensitive to the needs of their students. Therefore, the good teacher is good because he/she does not seem to be dominated by a narcissistic self which demands a spotlight out of a neurotic need for power and authority. Hamachek (1969) states:

".. . that good teachers are in a sense, 'total' teachers. . . . they seem able to be what they have to be to meet the demands of the moment. They seem able to move with the shifting tides of their own needs, the students, and do what has to be done to handle the situation" (p. 343).

Self-Fulfilling Prophecies

As a result of past experiences, individuals develop certain expectancies about their behaviors. Through the years individuals have been reinforced in their expectancies by their own evaluations of their behavior, their estimate of selves in relation to others, and their impressions of others' feelings toward them. In a review of the literature relative to the effects of expectancies of self and others on actual behavior, Brickman (1966) derived the two generalizations: 1) People who expect to fail are more likely to fail even when they succeed and desire success, and 2) If people do perform well, they are more likely to discount the evidence of their successes. Brickman believes that this occurs because behaviors that disconfirm expectations lead an individual to feel dissatisfied and uncomfortable. As a result, individuals desire to live up to their own expectations.

Research (Star, 1959; Poser, Dunn and Smith, 1964; and Guskin, 1967) indicates that expectations developed in early phases of a relationship lead persons to develop certain expectations about others and about their relationships with others. Therefore, early experiences in a relationship lead to relatively lasting effects and tend to lead to self-fulfilling phrophecies. Newcomb (1947) states that individuals, especially when their early encounters are experienced as unpleasant, tend to

90

withdraw from further interactions with others. As a consequence of this withdrawal, early impressions are not checked against future interactions and individuals tend to distort the behavior of others to fit these first impressions or perceptions. Therefore, individuals continually build up negative or positive impressions of the other which go unchecked. As a result, early expectations are maintained and future interactions are interpreted so as to reinforce these expectations.

Havelock (1971) suggest that in order to break this vicious cycle, interventions which encourage or force continued interactions may create new perceptions. He continues that additional interactions and feedback probably have the effect of creating a common ground for understanding and might create greater attraction through the continuous interaction.

The process of perceiving which precedes expectations, is unique to each individual. Bruner (1958) states that humans tend to maintain a consonance of their opinions, ideas and attitudes. Therefore, individuals attempt to eliminate or minimize surprise by imposing a subjective consistency upon their environments which is called a set. Zalkind and Costello (1969) identified four possible ways in which humans may distort their perceptions; these are stereotyping, the halo effect, projection and perceptual defense.

Principal-teacher, teacher-teacher, and student-teacher relations may be affected by their stereotyped perceptions of each other. Each may perceive the other as being more or less dependable than self or as superior or inferior in emotional characteristics and interpersonal relations. For example, an older teacher may view a younger teacher as an uncommitted professional who is not as conscientious as teachers of his/her generation. On the other hand, younger teachers may view older teachers or administrators as professionals who are not aware of the younger generation's needs. These perceptions may influence interactions and result in poor working relationships.

Another set or consistency in perceptions is the halo effect which refers to the process of perceiving favorably or unfavorably certain traits that are screened by the halo. A child who is punctual in completing assignments and helpful in the classroom may be perceived by the teacher as a good student and given high grades while the child who misses handing in an assignment and "acts up" occassionally may be perceived by the teacher as a poor student and given lower grades.

Projection is another set that enters into one's perceptions and expectations of others. Through projection, a person relieves his/her feelings of guilt or failure by projecting blame on someone else. Teachers who feel upset because of their inability to encourage a child in learning a concept may judge the child to be upset. Administrators who were unable to complete reports due to procrastination may perceive the faculty as a group that often fails to bring closure to tasks or decisions.

A fourth set that influences perceptions involves perceptual defense, the distortion of data so as to eliminate inconsistency. The teacher may select those factors which support his/her stereotyped impressions of a child or fellow teacher. Teachers who expect hostility in a disliked peer will selectively perceive much of the person's behavior as hostile and focus on these behaviors in order to maintain consistency.

Braun (1973) states that the psychological credibility of the self-fulfilling phenomenon is perhaps one reason that research has continued despite the failure of Rosenthal and Jacobson to provide totally convincing evidence. Neither Snow (1969) nor Thorndike (1965) deny the fact that teacher expectation may be a powerful force. Additional impetus has been provided by studies lending support to the phenomenon (Brophy and Good, 1970; Mendoze, et.al., 1971; and Sever, 1971).

92

Needs

Another psychological characteristic that is pervasive in a teacher's psychological structure is the concept of needs. Generally, needs refer to a teacher's basic desires, motives and drives. This concept has been used to describe broad areas as the need for food, clothing and shelter, the need for consistency in one's self-image, or the need for particular courses in order to obtain an education (Havelock, 1971). Needs such as hunger and self-consistency are considered extremely important and an integral part of a teacher's psychological structure. The need for particular courses, however, could be considered as relatively unimportant in its effect on one's psychological posture.

Maslow (1954) presents a need hierarchy which includes as the most basic, powerful need, the need for physical survival. In our society, the basic physical needs are fairly well satisfied in school faculty. Once these physical needs are satisfied, the safety needs emerge. Included in these safety needs are feelings of security. The insecure teacher, one whose safety needs are not met, has almost a compulsive need for order and stability and generally avoids anything different and unexpected (Goble, 1970). In contrast, the secure teacher, though still seeking some order and stability in his/her life, has a curiosity in the new and mysterious. Helping teachers feel physically safe or secure with their peers within the school environment is extremely important if teachers are to be flexible in their interactions.

Goble (1970) discusses the love and belonging needs identified by Maslow (1954) as finding a place within a group and establishing mutual trust. Mutual trust among teachers and among teachers and students involves the dropping of defenses and a lack of fear. When teachers' love and belonging needs are met, they feel free to be themselves and to interact with others in an accepting, open manner. When discussing the esteem needs, Maslow categorizes them as self respect and esteem from

others. Self-esteem includes such needs as desire
for competence, adequacy, achievement, independence,
and freedom. Respect from others includes such
concepts as recognition, acceptance and appreciation. Mutual respect and mutual trust are extremely important between teachers if schools are to
provide an environment that facilitates optimum
growth and development. Only when a trust base
has been established are teachers able to share.

Sharing is basic to establishing a school
atmosphere based upon humane relations. True sharing among teachers requires that they are concerned
with reaching toward the higher order needs identified by Maslow (1954) as self actualization and
the need to know and understand. The self actualization needs interpreted by Goble (1970) include
growth development, utilization of potential or
". . . the desire to become more and more what one
is, to become everything that one is capable of
becoming" (p. 41). The desire to know and understand includes the need to look for relations and
provide meanings and to construct a system of
values. If indeed schools are to provide a sharing
experience for teachers, then all involved must
attempt to create conditions conducive to true
sharing. According to Goble (1970), Maslow mentions environmental or social conditions in our
society that are prerequisites to basic need satisfaction. These conditions, necessary if a school
atmosphere of humane relationships is to become a
reality, include the freedom to speak, freedom to
do what one wishes as long as no harm is done to
others, freedom of inquiry, freedom to defend
oneself, honesty, fairness, order, and challenge
(stimulation). A school environment that exempli-
fies these characteristics would certainly facilitate learning and growth among all who interact.

Dobson and Dobson (1976) state that; 1) the
human is the center of the educational process,
and 2) by focusing on human needs, wants and desires a positive learning climate will flourish.
They continue that humans need to be needed, that
humans of all ages need to feel that they are

94

making meaningful contributions. A basic want of
human beings postulated by Dobson and Dobson focuses
on the premise that children and adults alike want
to be accepted, to feel that they belong or have
a place within the group. A basic desire of human
beings is to be free, independent or autonomous.
They state that humans have the potential for making
responsible decisions that enhance their unique
selves. When humans experience a sense of autonomy,
then and only then are they truly willing to cooperate with others without selfish motives. The
person who feels independence becomes aware of the
interdependence of all living things.

SUMMARY

1. Schools are complex social organizations and,
   therefore, simplistic approaches to improving
   the quality of schools are ineffective.

2. Any revolution in education will necessarily
   involve introducing the unique person of the
   teacher into the classroom.

3. A teacher's philosophy, personal values and
   beliefs form the foundation from which he/she
   makes choices and decisions for living life.

4. The "self as instrument" concept relative to
   teaching means that teacher effectiveness is
   a personal matter of the effective use of a
   unique self.

5. The person of the teacher is the most important
   factor in the learning process.

6. Value-neutrality on the part of the teacher is
   an impossibility. Therefore, teachers must be
   aware of the values they espouse.

7. Since teachers expose their values in interactions with others and since value collisions
   are inherent in a pluralistic society, then
   means for challenging teachers toward values/
   behavior congruency are needed.

8. The sensitivity of the teacher to self and
   others not only influences the communication

processes within the classroom but also the teacher's own personal growth.

9. The concept of self serves as a guide and mediator of perceptions, thoughts and actions. Therefore, the image a teacher has of self is of utmost importance.

10. Effective teachers are those who are human in the fullest sense.

11. Humans tend to maintain a consonance of their opinions, ideas and attitudes. Therefore, individuals attempt to eliminate or minimize surprise by imposing a subjective consistency upon their environments.

12. True sharing among teachers requires that they are concerned with reaching toward the higher order needs identified by Maslow.

13. When teachers experience a sense of autonomy, then they are willing to cooperate with others without selfish motives.

REFERENCES

Allport, G. W. Personality: A psychological in-
    terpretation. New York: Holt, Rinehart and
    Winston, 1937.

Anderson, G. and Walgerg, H. Classroom climate
    and group learning. 1967, ERIC Number ED
    015 156.

Beniskos, J. M. The person teacher. Education
    Digest. 1971, 36, 34-36.

Biddle, B. J. and Ellena W. J. Contemporary re-
    search on teaching effectiveness. New York:
    Holt, Rinehart and Winston, 1964.

Braun, C. Johnny reads the cues: Teacher expec-
    tation. The Reading Teacher, 1973, 26, 704-
    12.

Brickman, P. Performance expectations and perfor-
    mance. Ann Arbor, Michigan: Research Center
    for Group Dynamics, December, 1966. Mimeo.

Brophy, J. E. and Good, T. L. Teachers' communi-
    cation of differential expectations for
    children's classroom performance: Some be-
    havioral data. Journal of Educational Psy-
    chology, 1970, 61, 365-74.

Bruner, J. S. Social psychology and perception.
    In Maccoby, T. M. Newcomb, and E. L. Hartley,
    (Eds.), Readings in social psychology. New
    York: Holt, Rinehart and Winston, Inc., 1958.

Carkhuff, R. R. and Berenson, B. G. Beyond coun-
    seling and therapy. New York: Holt, Rinehart
    and Winston, Inc., 1967.

Childress, B. and Dobson R. Elementary teachers'
philosophies of human nature and students'
perceptions of the elementary school. Journal
of the Student Personnel Association for Teacher Education, 1973, 11, 153-61.

Combs, A. W. An educational imperative: The human
dimension. Washington, D.C.: National Education Association, 1970.

Combs, A. W., et.al. Florida studies in the help-
ing professions. Social Science Monograph,
Number 27. Gainsville: University of Florida
Press, 1969.

Combs, A. W. The professional education of teachers.
Boston: Allyn and Bacon, 1965.

Combs, A. W. (Ed.). Perceiving, behaving, becoming. Washington, D.C.: Association of Supervision and Curriculum Development, 1962.

Dahms, A. M. Emotional intimacy. Boulder, Colorado: Pruett Publishing Company, 1972.

Davidson, H. H., and Lang, C. Children's perceptions of their teachers' feelings toward them
related to self-perception, school achievement
and behavior. Journal of Experimental Education, 1960, 29, 107-18.

deBruin, H. C. Personality concept in relation
to quality teaching. Education, 1969, 89,
241-43.

Dewey, J. The influence of Darwin on philosophy.
New York: H. Holland Company, 1910.

Dieken, E. H. and Fox, R. B. Self-perceptions of
teachers and their verbal behavior in the
classroom. Educational Leadership. 1973, 30,
445-49.

Dobson, J., Grey, B., and Dobson, R. The effects of teacher-counselor consultation on the socio-metric status and achievement of elementary school children. Resources in Education. ED 172 103, November, 1979.

Dobson, J. The third force teacher: A profile. Forum on Open Education. Athens, Georgia: College of Education, The University of Georgia, 1976, 4, 24-29.

Dobson, R. L. and Dobson, J. Humaneness in schools: A neglected force. Dubuque, Iowa: Kendall/Hunt, 1976.

Dobson, R., Dobson, J., and Grahlman, W. F. Human emotions/feelings. In N. Colangelo, C. H. Foxley and D. Dustin (Eds.). Multicultural Nonsexist Education: A Human Relations Approach. Dubuque, Iowa: Kendall/Hunt, 1979, 47-58.

Dobson, R., Hopkins, S., and Elsom, B. Elementary teachers' philosophies of human nature and nonverbal communication patterns. Journal of the Student Personnel Association for Teacher Education, 1973, 11, 98-101.

Dobson, R., Sewell, R., and Shelton, J. Congruence of verbal and nonverbal behavior of elementary school teachers with differing beliefs about the nature of man. Journal of the Student Personnel Association for Teacher Education, 1974, 12, 157-64.

Durant, W. The story of philosophy. New York: Simon and Shuster, 1953.

Engel, M. The stability of the self-concept in adolescence. Journal of Abnormal Social Psychology, 1959, 58, 211-15.

Fisher, C., Mariave, R., and Filby, N. Improving teaching by increasing academic learning time. Educational Leadership, 1979, 37, 52-54.

Getzels, J. H. and Jackson, P. W. The teacher's personality and characteristics in H. L. Gage, (Ed.), Handbook of research on teaching. Chicago: University Press, 1963.

Glock, M. D. Is there a pygmalion in the classroom? The Reading Teacher, 1972, 25, 405-08.

Goble, F. The third force. New York: Grossman Publishers, 1970.

Good, T. Teacher effectiveness in the elementary school: What we know about it now. Journal of Teacher Education. 1979, 30, 52-64.

Good, T., Biddle B., and Brophy, J. E. Teachers make a difference. New York: Holt, Rinehart and Winston, 1975.

Goodlad, J. The trouble with humanistic education. Address given at the Fourth National Conference on Humanistic Education, West Georgia College, Carrollton, Georgia, April, 1977.

Gordon, T. T.E.T. New York: David McKay Company, Inc., 1974.

Guskin, A. E. The federal manager and research. Ann Arbor, Michigan: Center for research on utilization of scientific knowledge, University of Michigan, 1967. Mimeo.

Hamachek, D. Characteristics of good teachers and implications for teacher education. Phi Delta Kappan, 1969, 50, 341-44.

Havelock, R. G. Planning for innovation through dissemination and utilization of knowledge. Ann Arbor, Michigan: Center for Research on Utilization of Scientific Knowledge Institute for Social Research, 1971.

Jersild, A. T. When teachers face themselves. New York: Bureau of Publications, Teachers College, Columbia University, 1955.

100

Katz, D. and Stotland, E. A preliminary statement to a theory of attitude structure and change. In S. Koch (Ed.), Psychology: A study of a Science, Vol. 3: Formulations of the person and the social context, New York: McGraw-Hill, 1959.

Kelley, E. C. The fully functioning self. In A. W. Combs (Ed.), Perceiving, behaving, becoming. Washington, D.C.: Association of Supervision and Curriculum Development, 1962.

Kelley, E. C. and Rasey, M. I. Education and the nature of man. New York: Harper and Brothers, 1952.

Kemp, C. G. Intangibles in counseling. Boston: Houghton Mifflin, 1967.

Maslow, A. H. Motivation and personality. New York: Harper and Row, 1954.

May, R. Man's search for himself. New York: New American Library, 1953.

Mendoza, S. M., Good, T. L. and Brophy, J. E. The communication of teacher expectancies in a junior high school. Paper read at the American Educational Research Association Conference, New York, 1971.

Moustakas, C. The authentic teacher. Cambridge, Mass.: Howard A. Doyle Publishing Company, 1967.

Newcomb, T. M. Autistic hostility and social reality. Human Relations, 1947, 1, 69-86.

Poser, E. G., Dunn, I. and Smith, R. M. Resolving conflicts between clinical and research teams. Mental Hospitals, 1964, 15, 278-82.

Powell, M. Research on Teaching. The Educational Forum, 1978, 62, 27-37.

Purkey, W. W. Inviting school success. Belmont, California: Wadsworth Publishing Company, Inc., 1978.

Purkey, W. W. and Avila, D. Classroom discipline: A new approach. The Elementary School Journal, 1971, 71, 325-28.

Purkey, W. W. Self-concept and school achivement. Englewood Cliffs, N.J.: Prentice-Hall, 1970.

Ragan, W. B. Modern elementary curriculum. New York: The Dryden Press, Inc., 1953.

Raskow, E., Airasian, P., and Madaus, G. Assessing school and program effectiveness: Estimating teacher level effects. Journal of Educational Measurement, 1978, 15, 15-21.

Rogers, C. R. Learning to be free. Pastoral Psychology, 1962, 13, 45-51.

Rosenshine, B. Recent research on teaching behaviors and student achievement. Journal of Teacher Education, 1976, 27, 61-54.

Rosenthal, R. and Jacobson, L. Pygmalion in the classroom: Teacher expectation and pupil's intellectual development. New York: Holt, Rinehart and Winston, 1968.

Russell, D. H. and Fea, H. R. Research on teaching reading. In N. L. Gage, (Ed.), Handbook of research on teaching. Chicago: University Press, 1963.

Sanders, A. and Sanders, J. Why Humanistic Education? Colorado Journal of Educational Research, 1978, 17, 13-14.

Schroder, H., Karlins, M., and Phares, J. Education for freedom. New York: John Wiley and Sons, Inc., 1973.

102

Seaburg, D. The four faces of teaching. Pacific Palisades, California: Goodyear Publishing Company, Inc., 1974.

Seaver, W. B. Effects of naturally-induced teacher expectancies on the academic performance of pupils in primary grades. Unpublished doctoral thesis. Champaign, Illinois: University of Illinois, 1971.

Sinclair, R. L. Elementary school educational environments: Measurement of selected variables of environmental press. Unpublished doctoral thesis. Los Angeles: University of California, 1968.

Snow, R. E. Unfinished Pygmalion. Contemporary Psychology, 1969, 14, 197-99.

Spinoza, B. De. Ethics, part four. Great Books of the Western World. Chicago: Encyclopeida Britannica, Inc., 1952.

Stark, F. B. Barriers to client-worker communication at intake. Social Casework, 1959, 40, 177-83.

Thorndike, R. L. Review of R. Rosenthal and L. Jacobson, pygmalion in the classroom. American Educational Research Journal, 1968, 5, 708-11.

Usher, R. and Hanke, J. The "third force" in psychology and college teacher effectiveness research at the University of Northern Colorado. Colorado Journal of Educational Research, 1971, 10, 2-9.

West, P. T. Self-actualization resolving the individual-organization conflict. Clearing House, 1972, 47, 249-52.

Withall, J. and Lewis, W. W. Social interaction in the classroom. In N. L. Gage (Ed.), Handbook of research on teaching. Chicago: University Press, 1963.

Wrightsman, L. S. Measurement of philsophies of
    human nature. _Psychological Reports_, 1964,
    14, 743-51.

Wyne, M. D., White, K. P., and Coop, R. H. _The_
    black self. Englewood Cliffs, N.J.: Prentice-
    Hall, 1974.

Zalkind, S. S. and Costello, T. W. Perceptions:
    Some research and implications for administra-
    tion. In L. L. Cummings and W. E. Scott, Jr.
    (Eds.), _Readings in Organizational Behavior_
    and Human Performance. Illinois: Richard D.
    Irwin, Inc., and The Dorsey Press, 1969.

CHAPTER V

PERCEPTUAL BASE LINE SYSTEM

The preceding chapters have provided the foundation for our proposal of the perceptual base line system as a tool to aid educators in making educational decisions concerning the day to day operation of the school. The person as teacher has been illuminated as central to the total process. We believe past activities at dealing with educational planning have reduced the significance of the person of the teacher to a mere technician's role--obviously, we believe this is incorrect. We see the teacher as a student of education, certainly more than one who practices teaching. There is a vast difference between developing and implementing a personal philosophy and studying how to increase one's role performance. The time to assign the deerved label of professional to teachers is long overdue.

Obviously the rather strong stance we have presented relative to these affairs is based on a set of assumptions. In establishing these assumptions we have drawn heavily from the work of Rubin, 1975; and Gilchrist and Roberts, 1971. The assumptions are as follows:

1. We profess that whatever people believe about human nature determines the nature of the institutions they create.

2. We believe that people desire to improve whatever they are doing and are capable of doing so when they exercise freedom of will. No one person owns another's freedom; therefore, it cannot be a gift to be given. However, freedom of will can be facilitated and encouraged.

105

3. Tasks that are a function of freedom are of a higher quality than tasks that are products of coercion.

4. We believe people can constructively reconsider their values and beliefs, their philosophies, and that this process can be facilitated, without controlling direction, by providing a framework or structure.

5. We believe people, old and young alike, can direct their own being (growth) in terms of rational beliefs.

6. We believe that rational (honest) examination of philosophic differences among members of a school can serve to accelerate collective institutional goals. In fact it can be argued that without honest examination there can be no collective goals. Without some degree of concensus, the certainty of a problem with commitment to goals exists.

7. We believe that time should be treated as a luxury as opposed to a commodity.

8. We believe basic philosophies should be ultimately celebrated by translation into educational activities.

9. We believe knowledge with human potential orientation (the ultimate of what humans are, what they can become) and knowledge of self in relation to others, is central to positive human interactions (teaching).

10. We believe the capacity to assist others in realizing their potentials is perhaps the greatest virtue of teaching and leadership.

11. We believe that the question, "What should be done with people?" is of far more significance than the question "What can be done to people?" The first question deals with encouraging freedom; the second deals with altering behavior. Educational

decisions are not immune from criteria of morality.

12. We believe that only through freedom can one grow automatically. Persons direct their own evolutions and consequently are responsible for their decisions.

13. We believe the critical forces in self-evaluation are will and desire; school leadership should be committed to this end.

14. We believe that at first self-directed growth will not necessarily contribute to institutional activities, but that in the long run it is a wise investment. A self-correcting individual and institution are far more efficient than one that wears out and constantly needs readjustments.

Facilitation of Awareness

The perceptual base line system is a process approach that focuses on the facilitation of awareness of an individual's degree of congruency between his/her beliefs and day to day operations in the school setting. Additionally, the system provides group data that allows an individual to compare his/her personal beliefs with the collective beliefs of colleagues.

The perceptual base line system is not designed to foster change, but to encourage self awareness, self acceptance, and harmony between self-reported beliefs and practices. Most individuals accept the idea that in relationships with a friend, spouse or relative there are times when one becomes more accepting in order to prevent serious conflicts. Developing even a little more acceptance of another's values and beliefs or a better understanding of another's belief base are self-modifications which can markedly alter an individual's relationship with others. In the perceptual base line system the focus is on the facilitation of awareness of teachers own beliefs and respect for the differing beliefs of their peers.

Since the perceptual base line system is a process planning technique (outcomes are not pre-determined) the assignment of an operational definition is difficult, if not impossible. The system will vary according to time, circumstances, place, and persons involved. This chapter is a description of the process. However, the recommended instrumentation has served as an adhesive to give the approach similar procedural structure in several school districts where it has been implemented. This structural approach that has emerged is discussed later in this chapter.

Usually educational decisions and planning are founded on base line data. In this approach information is obtained through some kind of needs assessment procedure (usually a questionnaire) designed to accommodate the needs of the institution being assessed as opposed to being sensitive to the persons within the institution. The participants (teachers and students) are viewed as role players in an ongoing drama instead of persons in the process. Base line data is role and institutional oriented; perceptual base line data is person oriented, consequently having philosophical-values, psychological, and emotional dimensions. As has been substantiated in this book, decisions about schooling are value statements; therefore, any effort at school improvement must begin with the values and beliefs of those involved. This neglected area of school improvement must be brought to the forefront if planning is to have any lasting effect.

The need assessment or base line data approach focuses on the role of teacher; and the perceptual base line focuses on the person of the teacher. The following is an attempt to contrast the two approaches.

Need Assessment Approach	Perceptual Base Line System
1. Obtains information about teachers' needs that will serve to enhance the role as determined by institutional goals.	1. Obtains information about personal beliefs and practices and provides teacher with this information.
2. Recommendations for school improvement are made to bring teaching skills up to standard as set by institution.	2. Individual is presented with personal data relative to educational beliefs and practices.
3. School objectives are established by institution.	3. Individual is encouraged to determine personal beliefs.
4. Content for implementation of in-service programs is selected and organized by representatives of the institution.	4. Individual plans personal program of self and professional growth.
5. Learning experiences are selected and organized by institutional representatives, usually supervisory personnel.	5. Individual and/or groups of individuals initiate, design, develop and implement active learning experiences.
6. An evaluation design is specified by institution.	6. Individual and/or groups of individuals revise and refine current activities.

Activities engaged in by persons according to the two approaches generally do not vary greatly. The emphasis is on priority of the person's beliefs over role needs. In the perceptual base line system approach the school leader opts for personal power over status power. In this posture the emphasis is on active involvement of individual persons in professional and personal growth opportunities. When persons are actively involved in learning experiences the knowledge acquired has personal meaning. The personal meaning is the catalyst for bringing about congruency between beliefs and practices. Knowledge disseminated to a passive victim will not fulfill this function.

Data Gathering Instruments

We have designed a strategy for planning and decision making that identifies the beliefs that collectively constitute a personal philosophy of education and also the variables necessary to create or establish a phenomenon called schooling. Our efforts with this strategy indicated the need to create a two part instrument entitled Part I: Educational Beliefs System Inventory and Part II: Educational Practice Belief Inventory. The instruments identify the degree to which persons are experiencing beliefs-praxis congruency between their professed beliefs and educational practices. The instrumentation is intended as a tool for dialogue and self assessment rather than a technique for evaluation. Copies of the two instruments are contained in Appendix A, scoring keys are found in Appendix B, and a key for interpreting scores is presented in Appendix C.

The Educational Beliefs System Inventory. The Educational Beliefs System Inventory (EBSI) is a 69 item inventory composed of statements clustered under the following sub-tests.

1. What do you believe about Human Nature?
2. What do you believe about Motivation?
3. What do you believe about the Conditions of Learning?
4. What do you believe about Social Learning?
5. What do you believe about Intellectual Development?
6. What do you believe about Knowledge?

7. What do you believe about Society?

Each sub-test contains equal number of statements from three distinct educational camps: 1) Behavioristic psychology - Idealism philosophy, 2) Cognitive psychology - Experimentalism philosophy and 3) Humanistic psychology - Existentialism philosophy. The teacher is asked to judged each statement from the viewpoint of "This is what I really believe," and not "This is how it is now." The possible response categories range from: 1) complete agreement, 2) moderate agreement, 3) uncertain, 4) moderate disagreement, and 5) complete disagreement. Each sub-test is designed to yield scores which correspond to the three particular educational camps. Chapter III dealt with a description of these three camps and the types of educational decisions and activities advocated by each of the three.

The instruments may be hand scored and graphed or machine scored and graphed. An S.P.S.S. (Statistical Package for the Social Sciences) computer program has been written along with a Fortran plotting program so that the answers may be recorded on a standard answer sheet. By recording the answers on these standard answer sheets, Fortran programs will score and graph the results.

An example of scoring sub-test 1 is: items 1-15 are five statements each pertaining to (A) Behaviorism - Idealism, (B) Cognitivism - Experimentalism, and (C) Humanism - Existentialism. Each item is rated by the teacher from 1 (complete agreement) to 5 (complete disagreement). The scores from each of the five statements are added together and divided by 5 to yield mean A, B, and C scores. This procedure is followed for all seven sub-tests and then the mean scores are combined and divided by 7 to arrive at A, B, and C mean scores for the total Educational Beliefs System Inventory instrument. The mean score is shown as sub-test 8. The results can then be graphed to give the teacher a pictorial view of his/her philosophical profile.

This same process is followed for the group by summing all of the teachers scores and arriving

at a mean group score. This enables teachers to
compare their individual scores with the group,
if they choose to do so.

The Educational Practice Belief Inventory.
The Educational Practice Belief Inventory (EPBI)
is a 69 item inventory composed of statements
clustered under the following sub-tests:

9. What do you believe about Instruction?
10. What do you believe about Curriculum?
11. What do you believe about Organization?
12. What do you believe about Content?
13. What do you believe about Materials and
    Resources?
14. What do you believe about Evaluation?

The instructions, scoring and graphing procedures for this instrument are the same as for
the EBSI. This instrument also yields a philosophical profile relative to the three educational philosophies; (A) Behaviorism - Idealism,
(B) Cognitivism - Experimentalism, and (C) Humanism - Existentialism. The mean score of sub-tests
9 through 14 are shown as sub-test 15 and the mean
score of sub-tests 1 through 7 and sub-tests 9
through 14 combined are shown as sub-test 16.

Validity and Reliability. The two instruments
have been validated by a jury of experts. This
jury was comprised of five professors with a thorough knowledge base. Reliability was achieved
through the use of Cronbach Alpha Internal Consistency Reliability Scale. The internal consistency
reliability for the total A, B, and C sub-tests
for the Educational Beliefs System Inventory are:
A = .858, B = .796, C = .820. The internal consistency reliability for the total A, B, and C
sub-tests for the Educational Practice Belief
Systems are A = .825, B = .846, C = .795. When
the two instruments were combined and considered
as a whole, the total reliability for the A, B,
and C sub-tests are: A = .917, B = .884, and
C = .896.

112

Profile. When the thirteen sub-tests are
plotted graphically, the teachers can judge for
themselves if their educational beliefs and practices are harmonious or in conflict with each
other and/or the group profile. Also, a prevailing educational philosophy for the individual and/
or the group can be identified.

The purpose of the profile is not to convince
a person, or for that matter a total faculty, to
change philosophic beliefs or teaching behaviors,
but hopefully it will inspire some thinking about
the personal and professional direction the person
or persons want to take. We believe the strength
of the instrument lies in the discussion that follows the reporting of results. If an individual
or the entire faculty are dissatisfied with the
results then certainly the instrumentation can be
used as a tool for planning as well as for decision making. The results of the instruments simply
do not allow for the ignoring of crucial philosophic issues.

Briefly, the profile is designed to give the
individual a graphic view of his/her educational
beliefs/practices according to three schools of
thought. Hopefully it will be useful as a tool
for dialogue and as a way of thinking about and
dealing with some of the everyday problems that
occur when people interact.

The individual who is experiencing belief/
practice harmony would be one whose profile shows
his/her beliefs closely aligned with practices.
This would be represented graphically by a flat
line or almost flat line on sub-tests 1-7 (educational beliefs) and on sub-tests 9-14 (beliefs
about educational practices). A strong belief
will be graphed with a flat line either toward
the top (complete disagreement) or near the bottom
(complete agreement). An individual whose profile
tends to be a flat line around the middle (3) merely exhibits uncertainty.

Figure 1 is an example of an individual and

school composite profile. A key, interpreting each sub-test, according to the three camps, is provided in Appendix C. The "A" scores represent Behaviorism - Idealism camp while the "B" scores represent Cognitivism - Experimentalism, and "C" socres that of Humanism - Existentialism.

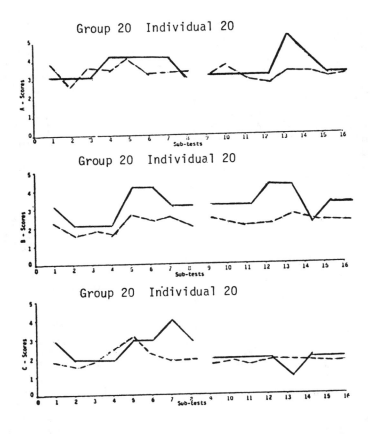

Figure 1.   Individual Profile, Sample

The EBSI and EPBI instruments provide each
individual with an A, B, and C profile. An example of an individual's profile is represented
in Figure 1 by the dark solid lines. Each person's score is determined and plotted and then a
group mean is determined for each sub-test. In
this way each individual can see where his/her
beliefs-practices are in relation to the group
as a whole. The group scores are seen in Figure
1 as a broken line superimposed over the individual scores.

In Figure 1, the "A" scores show general disagreement with Behavioristic beliefs and complete
disagreement with Behavioristic practice concerning
materials and resources (sub-test 13). The group
profile fluctuates from agreement with sub-test
2 (Motivation) to disagreement with sub-test 5
(Intellectual Development). The group practice
profile mainly indicates uncertainty in both
theory and practice.

The "B" scores in Figure 1 indicate agreement with Cognitive psychology and Experimentalism
philosophy in sub-test 2 (Motivation), 3 (Conditions of Learning), and 4 (Social Learning). This
individual disagrees with Cognitive psychology
and Experimentalism philosophy on sub-tests 5
(Intellectual Development) and 6 (Knowledge). In
practice, there is disagreement on sub-tests 12
(Content) and 13 (Materials and Resources) but
agreement on sub-test 14 (Evaluation). The
group profile reveals that as a whole, the
teachers' beliefs and practices closely follow
Cognitive psychology and Experimentalism philo-
phy.

Discussions with this individual teacher may
focus primarily on clarifying educational beliefs.
This teacher indicated uncertainty in his/her beliefs concerning human nature (sub-test 1) relative
to each of the basic camps. The composite scores
for the EBSI (sub-test 8) also indicate uncertain
position. Profile A indicates that the teacher
is uncertain or in moderate disagreement with

Behavioristic psychology and Idealism philosophy in both theory and practice. However, Profiles B and C indicate a blending of Cognitive psychology and Experimentalism philosophy with Humanistic psychology and Existential philosophy in educational beliefs. In practice, however, the individual tends to be in moderate or total agreement with Humanistic psychology and Existential philosophy.

The group profiles also indicate that the teachers tend to blend Cognitive Psychology and Experimentalism with Humanism and Existentialism in educational beliefs and practices. However, they seem to align themselves more closely with Cognitive Psychology and Experimentalism in educational beliefs.

As we stated earlier, these are possibilities based on observations of a graph. Hopefully during the human-social process of person-to-person interaction, other suggestions, possibilities and alternatives would surface and give rise to further exploration and eventual satisfaction, beliefs/ practice congruency.

An example of the general procedure that we follow in implementing the perceptual base line system follows:

Schedule of Meetings

Phase I   Objective 1. To meet with entire faculty to explain and answer questions relative to perceptual base line system.

Objective 2. To administer Educational Beliefs System Inventory and Educational Practice Beliefs Inventory.

Phase II   Objective 1. To report results, both individual profiles and total school profile, to faculty.

116

Objective 2. To provide appropriate materials to faculty explaining the meaning of scores relative to each subtest.

Phase III   Objective 1. To meet with entire faculty to discuss in detail what various philosophic bases resemble in day-to-day school practices.

Objective 2. To provide faculty with educational materials to supplement the explanation.

Phase IV   Objective 1. To hold interviews with each faculty member and discuss personal and professional implications of his/her profile.

Objective 2. To assist individuals in establishing goals for personal continuing education.

Phase V   Objective 1. To meet with administration and/or faculty representatives for the purpose of determining staff development activities based on needs, desires, and concerns of individual persons as expressed in Phase IV.

Objective 2. Design a plan for staff development.

Phase VI   Objective 1. Determine delivery strategies (briefings, conferences, workshops, seminars, travel, independent study, etc.) most suitable for staff development plan.

Objective 2. Implement staff development program.

As a consequence of implementing the program outlined above, we have arrived at the following conclusions:

1. Teacher-reported belief bases do shift.

This shift may be due to a change in philosophy or it may be due to a greater awareness of personal existing philosophy.

2. Classroom practices of persons are flexible according to their identified philosophy of education.

3. Teachers can make sound educational decisions relative to day-to-day operations in accordance with an educational philosophy.

4. Educational decisions made by teachers using the perceptual base line data are more sound than those based in scientific objectivity.

5. Teachers can function in a decision making capacity without superordinate directions and a scientific model to follow.

A Concluding Comment

In writing this book we have focused on the person as central to the role of teacher. We have examined and voiced our opinions about teachers as the unused experts in educational planning and decision making. Based on our beliefs about teachers as persons first of all, we provided a strategy for implementing our beliefs. Certainly we do not offer the strategy as a panacea but as a modest option to be used to illuminate the person of the teacher. We believe this illumination will make school a better place for boys and girls; a place where children can realize their potentials for loving, creating, growing, and knowing. To this end this book is committed.

REFERENCES

Gilchrist, R. and B. Roberts. *Curriculum development: A humanized systems approach.* Belmont, California: Fearon Publishers, 1974.

Rubin, L. (Ed.). *Improving in-service education: Proposals and procedures for change.* Boston: Allyn and Bacon, Inc., 1971.

APPENDIX A

EDUCATIONAL BELIEFS SYSTEM INVENTORY

PART I

Russell Dobson
Judith Dobson
W. Frank Grahlman
John Kessinger

Oklahoma State University

The reader is due an explanation about sexism problems related to this instrument. Most sensitive persons are aware of the problems of sexism in our society, terms which take the place of the generic use of "man," "mankind," and the pronoun "he" are awkward to use in a work of this nature. Terms are used in order not to unduly distort ideas. We hope the reader will understand the dilemma of the writers.

EDUCATIONAL BELIEF SYSTEM INVENTORY
PART I

Following is a list of 69 statements concerning various aspects of educational theory. Please judge each of the statements according to the scale below. In making your judgments, <u>DO NOT</u> consider each statement from the viewpoint, "This is how it is now." Rather, <u>DO CONSIDER</u> "This is what I really believe."

1 = complete agreement
2 = moderate agreement
3 = uncertain
4 = moderate disagreement
5 = complete disagreement

What do you believe about man?

1. Man can be characterized clearly in terms of his behavior.   1 2 3 4 5

2. Man's behavior is based on cognition, the act of knowing or thinking about a situation and not on the situation itself.   1 2 3 4 5

3. Man is greater than the sum of his parts.   1 2 3 4 5

4. Man is a malleable and passive reactor to his environment.   1 2 3 4 5

5. Man is best described in relative terms according to time, circumstance, and place.   1 2 3 4 5

6. Man is a social being and seeks to identify through interaction with others.   1 2 3 4 5

7. Man has an inherent tendency toward self-actualization and productivity.   1 2 3 4 5

8. Man's behavior is predictable.   1 2 3 4 5

9. Man's characteristics can be
   studied independently of one
   another.   1 2 3 4 5

10. Man can only be studied as
    a whole.   1 2 3 4 5

11. Individual perceptions are
    the only reality known to man.   1 2 3 4 5

12. Man is an active organism
    that develops goal-seeking
    potential.   1 2 3 4 5

13. Man's significance is deter-
    mined by the work he performs
    which is motivated by the
    promise of reward.   1 2 3 4 5

14. Freedom for an individual
    means growth and the willing-
    ness to change when modifi-
    cations are needed.   1 2 3 4 5

15. Man defines his own human
    potential through choices.   1 2 3 4 5

                                     A   B   C

                        Score   ___ ___ ___

What do you believe about
motivation?

16. Reinforcement (reward) must
    follow immediately after the
    desired behavior and be
    clearly connected with that
    behavior in the mind of the
    learner for learning to occur.   1 2 3 4 5

17. Behaviors which are reinforced
    (rewarded) are likely to recur.   1 2 3 4 5

18. Cognitive processes are set
    into motion (thinking) when
    the learner encounters an obsta-
    cle, difficulty, puzzle or

126

challenge in a course of action
which interests him.   1 2 3 4 5

19. Children are naturally curious
and will explore their sur-
roundings without adult inter-
ference and encouragement.   1 2 3 4 5

20. Children will create tasks that
are of educational significance
and structure methods of accomp-
lishing these tasks when given
the freedom to do so.   1 2 3 4 5

21. Productive learning experiences
require active involvement.   1 2 3 4 5

22. Learning occurs best when the
purposes and needs are realistic, meaningful and useful
to the learner.   1 2 3 4 5

23. Appropriate external stimulation of the learner is neces-
sary for optimal achievement.   1 2 3 4 5

24. Frequency of repetition is
necessary in acquiring skills
and in bringing about over-
learning to guarantee retention.   1 2 3 4 5

25. True learning occurs when the
experience is internalized.   1 2 3 4 5

26. The desire to learn comes from
within the individual.   1 2 3 4 5

27. Productive learning takes place
when the tasks are adjusted to
the maturity and experiential
background of the learners.   1 2 3 4 5

                                        A   B   C
                          Score   ___   ___   ___

What do you believe about the
conditions of learning?

28. The mind consists of seperate,
but related faculties which can
be trained. There is automatic
transfer of training.　　　　　1 2 3 4 5

29. If a child is absorbed with and
enjoying an activity, learning
is occurring.　　　　　　　　　1 2 3 4 5

30. Confidence in self influences
learning. The stage of development of the child affects the
degree of participation or
involvement in learning tasks
as well as mastery of skills.　1 2 3 4 5

31. The educative process begins
with providing the learner with
a smorgasboard of activities
that fit his/her stage of
development and which reflects
his/her concerns and interests.　1 2 3 4 5

32. Children are perceptually
closer to the learning situation than are teachers: subsequently, they see and feel
what is needed and are capable
of self-direction.　　　　　　1 2 3 4 5

33. Learning is largely a reactive
experience.　　　　　　　　　1 2 3 4 5

34. Learning occurs best when
competition for rewards among
learners is induced.　　　　　1 2 3 4 5

35. Learning processes proceed
best when the learner sees results, has knowledge of his
status and progress, achieves
insight, and gains understanding. 1 2 3 4 5

36. Man's mind is an information
receptacle which can produce
factual content mastery.　　　1 2 3 4 5

37. Learning emerges in the flow and continuity of man's total experiencing and growing.   1 2 3 4 5

38. Expectations made of the learner should be based upon knowledge of his abilities which are determined by physiological and social development.   1 2 3 4 5

39. Children are best taught exploratory behavior when threat is not present.   1 2 3 4 5

                                        A   B   C

Score   ___   ___   ___

What are your beliefs concerning social learning?

40. Children receive many satisfactions from work and stimulation from reasonable new challenges.   1 2 3 4 5

41. The purpose of the school is to prepare children for adulthood so they can assume a contributing role in society.   1 2 3 4 5

42. When man chooses he chooses for all men.   1 2 3 4 5

43. When groups of individuals act for a common goal there is better cooperation and more friendliness than when individuals in groups are engaged in competition with one another.   1 2 3 4 5

44. Behavior is a social product.   1 2 3 4 5

45. Satisfaction in learning is affected by the group atmosphere as well as the products.   1 2 3 4 5

46. Man has the capacity to adopt, adapt, and reconstitute present and past ideas and beliefs. He also has the capacity to invent.   1 2 3 4 5

47. Man creates his own environment.   1 2 3 4 5

48. Man creates groups which agree with his own reality.   1 2 3 4 5

49. Children should be motivated to learn what is significant and contributory to their lives.   1 2 3 4 5

50. Man is a social being who seeks active involvement with others.   1 2 3 4 5

51. Self-concept is observable through one's behavior or performance.   1 2 3 4 5

A   B   C

Score ___ ___ ___

What do you believe about intellectual development?

52. People possess different levels and amounts of intelligence. These can be ascertained and reported by a score derived from testing.   1 2 3 4 5

53. The normal curve expresses the social and academic expectation of where people are supposed to fit for the goodness of all.   1 2 3 4 5

54. Readiness for learning is a complex interplay of social, physiological, emotional and intellectual development.   1 2 3 4 5

55. The less planned adult intervention, the greater intellectual gains of the child.   1 2 3 4 5

130

56. Increase in intelligence tests scores are positively related to aggressiveness, competitiveness, initiative, and strength of felt need to achieve.　　　1 2 3 4 5

57. Learning involves creating relationships. Intellectual development proceeds from "wholes" to "parts" or from a simplified whole to more complex wholes.　　　1 2 3 4 5

　　　　　　　　　　　　　　　　　　A　　B　　C
　　　　　　　　　　　　Score ___ ___ ___

What do you believe about knowledge?

58. Knowledge is a model created by the individual that makes sense out of encounters with the external conditions in the environment.　　　1 2 3 4 5

59. Truth exists prior to the learning of it.　　　1 2 3 4 5

60. Knowledge is temporary and conditional.　　　1 2 3 4 5

61. Information becomes knowledge when it is perceived as relevant to the solutions of a particular problem.　　　1 2 3 4 5

62. Little or no knowledge exists which is necessary for all humans to possess.　　　1 2 3 4 5

63. Truth can be known for itself and not merely for some instrumental purposes.　　　1 2 3 4 5

　　　　　　　　　　　　　　　　　　A　　B　　C
　　　　　　　　　　　　Score ___ ___ ___

What do you believe about society?

64. Society is a process in which individuals participate.

1 2 3 4 5

65. The school preserves social order and builds new social orders when the public decides they are needed.

1 2 3 4 5

66. Mankind is made man by cultural birth.

1 2 3 4 5

67. Society is self renewing.

1 2 3 4 5

68. The way to improve civilization is by improving the quality of individuals, not by improving institutions.

1 2 3 4 5

69. Society has existence in man's minds.

1 2 3 4 5

A   B   C

Score ___ ___ ___

TOTAL SCORE   A___ B___ C___

EDUCATIONAL PRACTICE BELIEF INVENTORY

PART II

Russell Dobson
Judith Dobson
W. Frank Grahlman
John Kessinger

Oklahoma State University

The reader is due an explanation about sexism problems related to this instrument. Most
sensitive persons are aware of the problems of
sexism in our society, terms which take the place
of the generic use of "man," "mankind," and the
pronoun "he" are awkward to use in a work of this
nature. Terms are used in order not to unduly
distort ideas. We hope the reader will understand the dilemma of the writers.

EDUCATIONAL PRACTICE BELIEF INVENTORY
PART II

Following is a list of 69 statements concerning various aspects of educational practice. Please judge each of the statements according to the scale below. In making your judgments, DO NOT consider each statement from the viewpoint, "This is how it is now." Rather DO CONSIDER "This is what I really believe."

1 = complete agreement
2 = moderate agreement
3 = uncertain
4 = moderate disagreement
5 = complete disagreement

What do you believe about instruction?

70. Ongoing assessment, immediate feedback and various reinforcement devices should be used to insure that students remain task oriented. 1 2 3 4 5

71. The study period should be organized through mutual agreement between teacher and pupils with each child knowing what is expected of him. 1 2 3 4 5

72. Children naturally set goals and enjoy striving. 1 2 3 4 5

73. Children receive many satisfactions from work, have pride in achievement, enjoy the process, and gain a sense of worthiness from contribution. 1 2 3 4 5

135

74. The teacher functions as a resource person to individuals and groups rather than as a taskmaster. 1 2 3 4 5

75. Transmission of verifiable facts which constitute universal skills is necessary. 1 2 3 4 5

76. The ends of instructional activities should be exemplified in explicit behavioral terms. 1 2 3 4 5

77. Children who understand and who are involved in what they are doing will create satisfactory methods for achieving educational tasks. 1 2 3 4 5

78. Learning activities should be provided on the basis of individual needs. 1 2 3 4 5

79. Diagnostic and prescriptive teaching are absolute necessities. 1 2 3 4 5

80. Heterogenous subgrouping for instructional purposes is recommended in certain skill development areas such as math and reading. 1 2 3 4 5

81. Children are capable of assuming responsibility for their behavior and academic growth. 1 2 3 4 5

82. Children desire to be released, encouraged and assisted. 1 2 3 4 5

83. The teacher should decide when it is time to pull loose ends of learning activities together before moving on to another aspect of that which is to be learned. 1 2 3 4 5

84. Management of children is
    necessary to ensure proper
    growth.   1 2 3 4 5

                                               A   B   C
                                Score   ___ ___ ___

What do you believe about
curriculum?

85. The curriculum is a predeter-
    mined body of content with
    highly defined and restricted
    delimitations.   1 2 3 4 5

86. Day-by-day lesson plan objec-
    tives must be well defined
    and specific.   1 2 3 4 5

87. The curriculum should emerge
    from each student.   1 2 3 4 5

88. In order to maintain balance
    in the curriculum, subject
    matter priorities should be
    determined on the basis of
    societal and personal needs.   1 2 3 4 5

89. There should be some system
    of articulation between units
    within a school, between
    schools, with school systems,
    and between states.   1 2 3 4 5

90. Curriculum content must be
    sequenced since there is a
    logical structural sequence
    to knowledge.   1 2 3 4 5

91. Due to individual educational
    needs the scope of the curric-
    ulum should be planned to in-
    clude a wide variety of unify-
    ing and pupil-speciality
    learning activities.   1 2 3 4 5

92. The curriculum should reflect as its source the chilren of that school.   1 2 3 4 5

93. The curriculum sequence and scope is best divided into segmented, isolated, and compartmentalized packages of knowledge specified by grade levels.   1 2 3 4 5

94. Elements of the curriculum should be derived from the substance of knowledge itself.   1 2 3 4 5

95. The curriculum is dynamic because of its constant emergence.   1 2 3 4 5

96. Curriculum structure exists largely in teachers and student heads, not on paper.   1 2 3 4 5

97. Though the curriculum has some degree of systematic structure, it should be flexible enough to capitalize on emergent learning situations.   1 2 3 4 5

98. Since the curriculum must be considered dynamic and forever emerging, each curriculum area should be subjected to continuous revision and evaluation.   1 2 3 4 5

99. The curriculum sequence in certain subject matter areas should be based on a spiral structure which permits the learner to conceptualize by moving from limited perceptivity.   1 2 3 4 5

	A	B	C
Scope	___	___	___

138

What do you believe about
organization?

100. The teaching function should
be one of diagnosing, prescribing, treating, analyzing
results and writing the next
prescription.   1 2 3 4 5

101. Individual differences should
be viewed as existing between
and among learners as opposed
to differences existing with-
in individual students.   1 2 3 4 5

102. The school should be organized
in such a way that it provides
opportunity for each student
to have a warm, personal relationship with competent teach-
ers.   1 2 3 4 5

103. The contributions of special-
ized personnel should be used
as students progress through
the school, but their work
should be coordinated with
and related to the total pro-
gram.   1 2 3 4 5

104. Internal coordination and
planning should result in the
utilization of special talents
and skills which a particular
teacher or group of teachers
may possess.   1 2 3 4 5

105. The organizational system
should permit coordination
and planning by groups of
teachers responsible for
clusters of children in both
large and small groups.   1 2 3 4 5

106. The horizontal organization of
the school should permit flexibility in assigning small and
large numbers of pupils to in-
structional groups.   1 2 3 4 5

107. Individual differences should
be acknowledged by the individual pacing of students through
prescribed study sequences.   1 2 3 4 5

108. The horizontal organization
of the school should permit
students to be assigned to
instructional groups on ability
within subject matter areas.   1 2 3 4 5

109. The organization of the school
should reflect a system where-
by each child must measure up
to a specific level of perfor-
mance.   1 2 3 4 5

110. The organizational structure
should not result in "labeling"
children at an early age.   1 2 3 4 5

111. The vertical organization of
the school should provide for
continuous unbroken, upward
progression of all learners,
with due recognition of the
wide variability among learners
in every aspect of their devel-
opment.   1 2 3 4 5

112. The organizational design of
the school should be an expression of the needs, wants, and
desires of its clientele.   1 2 3 4 5

113. The organization should provide
for the interdisciplinary na-
ture of education.   1 2 3 4 5

114. Children should not be grouped
according to ability.   1 2 3 4 5

                                            A   B   C

                               Score ___ ___ ___

What do you believe about
content?

115. The content of any education
program must reflect predetermined survival skills necessary for life.   1 2 3 4 5

116. Content should contribute to
the achievement of educational
objectives or to the mission of
the school.   1 2 3 4 5

117. There is little information
that all should be required
to know.   1 2 3 4 5

118. Sequence in content should
reflect a logical structural
sequence to knowledge and to
development.   1 2 3 4 5

119. One creates knowledge through
personal integration of experience. Therefore, one's knowledge does not categorize into
separate disciplines.   1 2 3 4 5

120. There should be a balance
between the content-centered
curriculum and the process
curriculum.   1 2 3 4 5

                           A   B   C

Score __ __ __

What do you believe about
materials and resources?

121. Centralized resource centers
should include materials com-
mensurate to the stages of
development reflected by the
students being served.   1 2 3 4 5

122. Emphasis should be placed on trade and reference works and on visual aids as opposed to strict textbook approach.   1 2 3 4 5

123. Materials that can be easily prescribed (programmed materials, teaching machines, subject matter programs, learning packets, and kits) are desirable.   1 2 3 4 5

124. Wide use should be made of raw materials.   1 2 3 4 5

125. Resources should be limited only by teachers' and students' imaginations.   1 2 3 4 5

126. There should be an emphasis on appropriate diagnostic aids.   1 2 3 4 5

                                  A   B   C

Score   ___ ___ ___

What do you believe about evaluation?

127. A uniform standards approach to evaluation fails to consider individual differences of children.   1 2 3 4 5

128. Evaluation programs should have three dimensions: a) quantitative measurements, b) teachers' judgment, and c) the child's perceptions.   1 2 3 4 5

129. Learning can be assessed intuitively by observing a child working or playing.   1 2 3 4 5

130. A pupil should be placed in a given learning environment based on a diagnosis that is best suited for his/her maturity, abilities attainment, and overall general nature.   1 2 3 4 5

142

131. Evaluation must be quantitative and qualitative to be of real value.　　　1 2 3 4 5

132. Objective means of measuring performance may produce negative consequences upon learning.　1 2 3 4 5

133. In evaluating, the teacher's description of what the child is doing should include all aspects of growth.　　　1 2 3 4 5

134. Pupils should be ranked in terms of other children.　　　1 2 3 4 5

135. Errors are an indispensable aspect of the learning process. Errors are expected and desired, for they contain feedback essential for continued learning.　　　1 2 3 4 5

136. Qualities of one's learning that can be meticulously assessed are not inevitably the most important.　　　1 2 3 4 5

137. Predetermined standards should apply to all students in a grade or school.　　　1 2 3 4 5

138. Academic standards should serve the purpose of excluding persons in the formal school program.　　　1 2 3 4 5

	A	B	C
Score	___	___	___

TOTAL SCORE A___ B___ C___

APPENDIX B

DIRECTIONS FOR SCORING
EDUCATIONAL BELIEFS SYSTEM INVENTORY AND
EDUCATIONAL PRACTICE BELIEF INVENTORY

The key to the philosophic direction of each statement included in each category follows:

1. Compute sum for each set of items (i.e. sum
    scores for A, B, C) in each category.

2. Divide sum by number of statements. For exam-
    ple, category 1 "What do you believe about
    Man" has 15 statements, 5 each for each of
    the three camps. So each set of 3 scores in
    this category would be divided by 5 to produce
    3 composite scores.

3. The scores indicate the degree of agreement or
    disagreement with each of the three camps rela-
    tive to the particular category.

EDUCATIONAL BELIEFS SYSTEM INVENTORY

What do you believe about man?

A. 1, 4, 8, 9, 13   Sum the scores for each
B. 2, 5, 6, 12, 14   set of items and divide
                          each of the three totals
C. 3, 7, 10, 11, 15   by 5 to arrive at A, B,
                          C scores.

What do you believe about motivation?

A. 16, 17, 23, 24   Sum the scores for each
B. 18, 21, 22, 27   set of items and divide
                          each of the three totals
C. 19, 20, 25, 26   by 4 to arrive at A, B,
                          C scores.

What do you believe about the conditions of learning?

A. 28, 33, 34, 36   Sum the scores for each
                          set of items and divide
B. 30, 31, 35, 38   each of the three totals
C. 29, 32, 37, 39   by 4 to arrive at A, B,
                          C scores.

What are your beliefs concerning social learning?

A. 41, 44, 49, 52   Sum the scores for each
                          set of items and divide
B. 40, 43, 45, 46   each of the three totals
C. 42, 47, 48, 50   by 4 to arrive at A, B,
                          C scores.

What do you believe about intellectual development?

A. 52, 53   Sum the scores for each
                          set of items and divide
B. 54, 56   each of the three totals
C. 55, 57   by 2 to arrive at A, B,
                          C scores.

What do you believe about knowledge?

A. 59, 63   Sum the scores for each
                          set of items and divide
B. 60, 61   each of the three totals
C. 58, 62   by 2 to arrive at A, B,
                          C scores.

What do you believe about society?

A. 65, 66   Sum the scores for each
                          set of items and divide
B. 64, 67   each of the three totals
C. 68, 69   by 2 to arrive at A, B,
                          C scores.

To arrive at composite scores for each of the three camps (Part I) sum the means for each of the three camps and divide by 7. The three scores (A, B, C) reflect the overall degree of agreement with beliefs of each of the camps.

EDUCATIONAL PRACTICE BELIEF INVENTORY

What do you believe about instruction?

A. 70, 75, 76, 79, 84   Sum the scores for each
B. 71, 74, 78, 80,·83   set of items and divide
                          each of the three totals
C. 72, 73, 77, 81, 82   by 5 to arrive at A, B,
                          C scores.

What do you believe about curriculum?

A. 85, 86, 90, 93, 94   Sum the scores for each
B. 88, 89, 91, 97, 99   set of items and divide
                          each of the three totals
C. 87, 92, 95, 96, 98   by 5 to arrive at A, B,
                          C scores.

What do you believe about organization?

A. 100, 101, 107, 108,   Sum the scores for each
   109   set of items and divide
                          each of the three totals
B. 103, 104, 106, 106,   by 5 to arrive at A, B,
   111   C scores.

C. 102, 110, 112, 113,
   114

What do you believe about content?

A. 115, 116   Sum the scores for each
B. 118, 120   set of items and divide
                          each of the three totals
C. 117, 119   by 2 to arrive at A, B,
                          C scores.

What do you believe about materials and resources?

A. 123, 126   Sum the scores for each
B. 121, 122   set of items and divide
                          each of the three totals
C. 124, 125   by 2 to arrive at A, B,
                          C scores.

What do you believe about evaluation?

A. 130, 134, 137, 138   Sum the scores for each
                           set of items and divide
B. 127, 128, 131, 133   each of the three totals
                           by 4 to arrive at A, B,
C. 129, 132, 135, 136   C scores.

To attain composite scores for each of the three
camps (Part II) sum the means for each of the
three camps and divide by 6. The three scores
(A, B, C) reflect the overall degree of agreement
with beliefs of each of the camps.

APPENDIX C

SUBTEST KEY

Each sub-test (1 through 16) yields an A, B and C score with A representing Behaviorism, B representing Cognitivism, and C representing Humanism. The scale is from complete agreement (a score of 1) to complete disagreement (a score of 5) pertaining to these philosophical beliefs. A score of 1 on sub-test A1 would indicate complete philosophical agreement with Behaviorism in what you believe about Man while a score of 5, on the same sub-test, would indicate the opposite (complete disagreement with Behaviorism regarding what you believe about Man).

Sub-test 8 gives an over-all A, B and C score on the EBSI (Educational Beliefs System Inventory). Sub-test 15 gives an over-all, A, B and C score on the EPBI (Educational Practices Belief Inventory). Sub-test 16 gives an over-all A, B and C score on all items (1 through 138), combinning the two instruments for a composite score.

The completed inventories yield a 48 dimension philosophical profile of the individual with regard to educational beliefs and educational practices.

The following interpretations are based on scores of 1 which indicate complete agreement. The degree of agreement can be ascertained by the score reported on each of the separate sub-tests.

Educational Belief System Inventory
Part I

Sub-test	Items	Topic
A1, B1, C1	1-15	What do you believe about Man?
A2, B2, C2	16-27	What do you believe about Motivation?

A3, B3, C3	28-39	What do you believe about the Conditions of Learning?
A4, B4, C4	40-51	What are your beliefs concerning Social Learning?
A5, B5, C5	52-57	What do you believe about Intellectual Development?
A6, B6, C6	58-63	What do you believe about Knowledge?
A7, B7, C7	64-69	What do you believe about Society?
A8, B8, C8	1-69	(This is a composite A, B and C score for the above 69 items)

Educational Practice Belief Inventory
Part II

A9, B9, C9	70-84	What do you believe about Instruction?
A10, B10, C10	85-99	What do you believe about Curriculum?
A11, B11, C11	100-114	What do you believe about Organization?
A12, B12, C12	115-120	What do you believe about Content?
A13, B13, C13	121-126	What do you believe about Materials and Resources?
A14, B14, C14	127-138	What do you believe about Evaluation?
A15, B15, C15	70-138	(This is a composite A, B and C score for the above 69 items)
A16, B16, C16	1-138	(This is a composite A, B and C score for all 138 items)

PART I

Sub-test

A1   Man's potential tends toward evil. There-
       fore, for the good of society and them-
       selves, children must be directed and
       controlled. These persons attempt to
       shape learners according to their values
       and teach them what they should know.

B1   A neutral belief of man is expressed.
       These persons begin with children where
       they are perceived to be functioning
       and manipulate the environment so that
       the children have the best possible ex-
       perience based on the adult's judgment
       of what is best. Human potential is
       seen as a goal to be realized. The
       total person is one who is in harmony
       with the external environment.

C1   Man is inherently inclined toward good-
       ness. Man is cooperative and constantly
       seeking experiences that enhance his/her
       unique self. Individual perceptions are
       the only reality known to man.

A2   Motivation is interpreted as the process
       of initiating, sustaining and directing
       the activities of the organism. Appro-
       priate external stimulation, usually in
       the form of rewards is necessary for
       optimal achievement.

B2   Focuses on a blend of the teacher as man-
       ipulator and the intellectual structures
       that characterize what is to be taught.

C2   Focuses on the person as the initiator
       of their own learning tasks. The most
       desirable rewards are internal in nature
       and are a reflection of self satisfaction.

A3 Focuses on training the separate faculties of the mind. Learning is largely a reactive experience, therefore learning situations should be created to induce competition for rewards among learners.

B3 Focuses on a combination of self confidence, physiological, social, and intellectual development in determining learner expectations. Also concerned with whether or not learning tasks are lifelike or functional. Concerned with the learner working up to his/her ability.

C3 Recognizes that the learner is perceptually closer to the learning situation than are teachers: subsequently, they see and feel what is needed and are capable of self-direction. Experiencing, being, and learning are seen as a totality that can be dichotomized only after the fact. Learning emerges in the flow and continuity of man's total experiencing and growing. There cannot be stated outcomes of learning.

A4 Social learning is seen as the gradual acquisition of attitudes and behavior that enable the individual to function as a member of society. Emphasis is on the development of behavior patterns which are acceptable to society.

B4 Focuses on how the individual functions relative to group norms. Satisfaction in learning is affected by the group atmosphere as well as the products.

C4 Accepts that man can create his/her own environment. Sees the person as central to their own idiosyncratic universe.

A5 Intelligence, is for the most part, a function of environmental conditions. Persons possess different levels and amounts of intelligence.

156

B5   Focuses as much on learning style as on
learning rate. Readiness for learning is
a complex interplay of social, physiological, emotional, and intellectual
development.

C5   Emphasizes that intellectual development
proceeds from "wholes" to "parts" or
from a simplified whole to more complex
wholes. Sees intellectual potential as
already existing within the individual
as opposed to a phenomenon to be developed or realized.

A6   Submits the existence of a central body
of knowledge that must be transmitted to
all. The truth is preexistent to the
learning of it. The test of truth is
its correspondence to reality.

B6   Emphasizes that knowledge is rooted in
experience. Knowledge is therefore tentative. As individuals and situations
change then what is true will also change.
Workability is the test of truth.

C6   Submits that the only thing a person can
be certain of is that they experience a
stream of thoughts and feelings. Truth
is an individual matter.

A7   Sees the function of schooling as pre-
serving social order and building new
social orders when the public has decided
they are needed (preservation of the
culture). The task of the school is to
develop a standardized student-citizen
as the product. Tendency is toward a
meritocratic society.

B7   Society is a process in which individuals
participate. The major role of the
school is to teach the adults of tomorrow
to deal with the planning necessarily involved in the process called society. Education must serve as a source of new ideas.

C7   Specifies that the way to improve society is through improving the quality of individuals, not through improving institutions. The school's primary task is individual; that is, the school should concentrate upon the development of absolute freedom in the child. The tendency is toward an egalitarian society.

A8   Composite score - Essentialism - Behaviorism

B8   Composite score - Experimentalism - Cognitivsm

C8   Composite score - Existentialism - Humanism

PART II

A9   Focus is on indoctrination. The transmission of verifiable facts is paramount. Instructional activities are preplanned with specific performance objectives clearly stated.

B9   The role of the teacher is seen as learning manager and consultant whose primary task is to orchestrate the learning environment.

C9   Instructional behavior of the teacher is determined by the learner and occurs only by invitation from the learner. Freedom of the learner is central to the instructional act.

A10   Curriculum is highly structured and content centered; it is predetermined and logical. It consists of a common core of subject matters, intellectual skills, and accepted values that are essential and are to be transmitted to all students.

B10   Future utility and unversalism are considered in the selection of content. The
sequencing of content is based on identified stages of development. Learning
experiences are generally problem centered.

C10   The curriculum is viewed as dynamic and
emergent and a consequence of the students
needs, wants, and desires. Each student
is seen as an unlimited reservoir of
curriculum.

A11   The organizational arrangement is rigid
and orderly in nature; emphasis is on
management and efficiency. Time-space
are segmental.

B11   Flexible scheduling is related to instructional needs of the staff. Individualized
instruction occurs by pacing the individual
through study sequences.

C11   Individual pupils plan their own use of
time within limits of personal and social
order. The organization provides for the
interdisciplinary nature of education; no
area of knowledge can exist independent
of all other areas of knowledge.

A12   The content is decided by the state. Suggests the desirability of a shared corpus
of content. The planners task is the
identification of common interests.

B12   Emphasis is on a balance between the
content-centered curriculum and the process curriculum.

C12   Concerned with process skills that enable
the person to know, to think, to value,
to feel, and to act. The quality of being
is more important than quality of knowing;
knowledge is a means of education, not
its end.

A13   Emphasis is on materials that correlate
       with a diagnostic approach and that can
       be easily prescribed such as programmed
       materials, teaching machines, subject
       matter programs, learning packets, and
       tests.

B13   Emphasis is on a wide range of materials
       and resources.

C13   Resources are limited only by teachers'
       and students' imaginations.

A14   Evaluation reveals itself in the form
       of measurement and is based on compari-
       sons and is product oriented. Evalua-
       tion standards and procedures are deter-
       mined by authority and imposed upon
       students.

B14   Focuses on what is learned and attempts
       to utilize this information in prescrib-
       ing future tasks. Attempts to evaluate
       critical thinking, problem solving, and
       higher order cognitive skills.

C14   Focuses on self evaluation. External
       feedback is available upon student re-
       quests and is a shared experience.

A15   Composite score for A Part II

B15   Composite score for B Part II

C15   Composite score for C Part II

A16   Total composite score

B16   Total composite score

C16   Total composite score

SUBJECT INDEX

Accountability, 5-7, 22

Back-to-basics movement, 6
Behaviorism, 43-45
Beliefs, 27
  personal, 73-80

Cognitive-field psychology, 47-48
Curriculum:
  add on, 2
  definition of, 57,64,66
  evaluation of, 65-66
  organization of, 65

Decisions, 31-32
  strategies of, 33-34

Education:
  definition of, 3
  purpose of, 56,62
Educatonal Beliefs System Inventory:
  interpretation of, 155-158
  profile, 113-116
  reliability, 112
  scoring, 147-148, 153-154
  sub-tests, 110-111, 123-132
  validity, 112
Educational Practice Belief Inventory:
  interpretation of, 155-160
  profile, 113-116
  reliability, 112
  scoring, 149-150, 154-155
  sub-tests, 112, 133-143
  validity, 112
Essentialism, 43, 45-46
Evaluation, 58, 67-66
Existentialism, 50, 53-54
Experimentalism, 49-50

Feelings:
  personal, 85-86

Human emotions, 57, 63-64
Human nature, 56,59

161

Human growth and development, 57, 62-63
Humanistic psychology, 50-54

Interpersonal interactions, 57, 63-64
Instructional behavior, 57, 64-65

Knowledge, 56, 60-61

Language of schooling, 54-66
Learning:
  nature of, 56, 59-60

Needs, 93-95
Needs assessment, 10, 108-110

Ownership of ideas, 10-11

Perceptual baseline:
  assumptions, 105-107
  facilitation of awareness, 107-110
  implementation of, 110-114
  premises, 11-13
  staff development, 110-118
Personal beliefs, 13-14
Personality characteristics, 88-90
Personhood, 21
Philosophy, 24-27, 32, 34-35
  personal, 74-86
Power, 29-30
Pragmatism, 47, 48-50
Psychological structure:
  personal, 86-95

Role:
  accessibility, 7-10
  behavior, 10

School:
  improvement and scientism, 3-5
  organization, 57, 65
Self concept, 57, 63, 87-88
Self fulfilling prophecies, 90-92
Sensitivity:
  personal, 84-86
Society:
  nature of, 56,61

Teacher:
  feelings, 85-86
  needs, 93-95

personality characteristics, 88-90
person of, 73-95
psychological structure, 86-95
self concept, 57, 63, 87-88
self fulfulling prophecies, 90-92
sensitivity of, 84-86
Teaching:
  as a job, 29
Training:
  definition, 3

Values:
  educational objectives, 24-27
  importance of, 21-24
  personal, 80-84